Gary D.
Erickson

The Conversion Experience

A Biblical Study of the
Blood, Water
and **Spirit**

The Conversion Experience

A Biblical Study of the
Blood, Water
and Spirit

The Conversion Experience:
A Biblical Study of
The Blood, Water and Spirit

By Gary D. Erickson

©1987 Word Aflame Press
  Hazelwood, MO 63042-2299
Reprint: 1994, 1995

Illustrated by Gary Erickson
Cover Design by Tim Agnew

All Scripture quotations in this book are from the King James Version of the Bible unless otherwise identified.

Printed in United States of America

Printed by

Library of Congress Cataloging-in-Publication Data

Erickson, Gary D., 1948-
     The conversion experience.

     1. Conversion—Biblical teaching.   2. Bible. N.T.—
Criticism, interpretation, etc.   I. Title.
BS2545.C59E75   1987   248.2'4   87-6157
ISBN 0-932581-13-7

Dedication

This work is dedicated to my wife, Judy, who is my best friend and confidant. Without her encouragement and patience it would not have been completed.

TABLE OF CONTENTS

5. The Tabernacle as God's Witness — *71*
   Israel's approach to God in the Old Testament, especially in atoning for sin, was through the Tabernacle and later the Temple. The approach to God involved blood at the brazen altar, water at the laver of water, and Spirit in the Holy Place. This is another beautiful type of our conversion experience.

6. The Natural Birth as God's Witness — *97*
   Jesus, the master teacher, used the natural birth as an analogy of our entrance into the kingdom of God. The inconveniences of pregnancy and the suffering in labor are compared to repentance. The infant is suspended in a watery world for nine months, which parallels baptism in water. At birth, the doctor looks for the breath of life and listens for the cry. Our Holy Ghost experience is the breath of life accompanied by the cry of speaking in other tongues.

7. The Miracle of the Seed as God's Witness — *109*
   Jesus said, "Except a corn of wheat fall into the ground and die, it abideth alone" (John 12:24). The germination process of a seed is another beautiful analogy of our conversion and of the Lord's death, burial and resurrection.

8. The Witness at Calvary — *119*
   The six hours Jesus hung on Calvary are climactic and laden with meaning. There we see the judgment of all sin for all time. John 19:34 and I John 5:8 tells of the blood and water that flowed from the side of Jesus. At Calvary itself there is the witness

of blood, water and Spirit.

Foreword

It's almost inexplicable! But God has always been a God of blood, water and Spirit. These terms are redemption language. Whenever the children of Israel made their famed exodus from Egypt it was under the blood of the lamb, through the water of the Red Sea, with the hovering glory cloud of the Spirit above them. The same is true in the Tabernacle—the blood at the altar, the water at the laver, and the eternal Spirit resident atop the mercy seat.

Jesus is the great exclamation point of this truth. "There are three that bear witness in earth, the Spirit, and the water, and the blood: and these three agree in one" (I John 5:8). He provided all three. When He died at Calvary, forthwith came blood and water. The Spirit descended on Him as a dove at River Jordan. On and on we could go. It was the message of Pentecost. "This same Jesus whom you crucified. . ."—that's the blood. "Repent and be baptized. . ."—there's the water. "And ye shall receive the Holy Ghost. . ."—that's the descending Spirit.

Pastor Gary D. Erickson has done a great work for the body of Christ in producing this manuscript. It is especially meaningful because not only is it useful to ministers of the gospel, but it is in layman's language. Any person can pick this up and read his way either into the truth or into a deeper knowledge of already-experienced truth.

Hasten into its pages and don't stop till you're finished. Congratulations to my friend the Reverend Gary Erickson, for a job well done and a need most assuredly met!

T. F. Tenney

11

Author's Preface

The most important issue facing mankind is how to be saved. That is what this book is about. It addresses the subject of entrance into the Christian church, frequently referred to as conversion.

Much of the book involves typology. I have attempted to base all types on strong biblical doctrine and New Testament example. Types give color and profile to abstract concepts, enhancing understanding and aiding in the communication of biblical truth, but are not in themselves the primary source of doctrine. My goal is not to construct a doctrine from types, but rather to provide reinforcement of biblical doctrine using tangible examples that illustrate the truth with beautiful harmony.

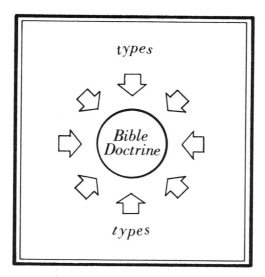

I have not explored all the treasures of this important subject, but I trust enough of its beauty is uncovered to motivate the reader to a further investigation. Neither our zeal for the doctrine about Christ nor our joy in an emotional experience with Christ should ever exceed our love and commitment to Jesus Christ Himself. We should never become so preoccupied with the mechanics that we forget the spirit of obedience.

1.

The Witness of Blood, Water and Spirit

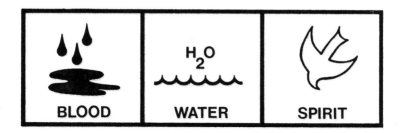

| BLOOD | WATER | SPIRIT |

"And there are three that bear witness in earth, the Spirit, and the water, and the blood: and these three agree in one" (I John 5:8).

God uses three elements—*blood, water* and *Spirit*—
to take us from the human known to the spiritual unknown.
The three witnesses named in I John 5:8 appear in the
work of Jesus Christ when He purchased our salvation.
They also clearly typify the process of our glorious transformation from a sinner to a child of God. The conversion
experience in our lives parallels the redemptive work of
Jesus, specifically His death, burial and resurrection.

The redemptive work of the Lord Jesus was a natural,
physical event. The blood He shed was red, warm blood
oozing forth from the ugly, torn flesh wounds of a real man.
It was a macabre sight, a painful and agonizing death. The
events of Calvary thunder through time with powerful force.
All the anguish and pain of Calvary grips our minds through
just the mention of Jesus' blood. That one word, *blood,*
when associated with our Lord, brings us joy when we consider what it accomplished and sorrow when we consider
His agony. But either emotion reminds us of its reality.

Joseph of Arimathea stumbled to assure his footing
as the weight of the corpse fell from the cross to his
shoulders. He had requested Pilate for permission to take
charge of this reverent task personally. With the aid of
Nicodemus, He wrapped Jesus' body in a linen cloth along
with aloes and myrrh. The dank darkness engulfed them
as they entered the freshly hewn tomb and labored to place
His body to rest with respect and dignity. Their hearts were

heavy with gloom due to the horrible madness of that afternoon. They strained against the heavy stone as it rolled into place over the mouth of the tomb. Even though His execution was sudden and no preparations were previously made, Jesus was buried respectfully in a new tomb. That the tomb was borrowed did not matter; He did not need it very long anyway!

The burial of Jesus was a physical event. It is historical and noteworthy, for it typifies a burial in our conversion experience. "We are buried with him by baptism into death" (Romans 6:4). This is the witness of *water.*

After the death and burial of Jesus, the disciples were frightened. As they hid behind closed doors, their minds burned with memories of Him. Their hearts throbbed with sorrow for the loss of His friendship and the security He provided. Bewilderment overcame them as they tried to decipher what had happened.

After many hours of secretly confiding together and after several sleepless nights, suddenly their numb and weary minds were electrified by the thought that perhaps He was alive. Peter and John raced to the tomb to find it really empty except for the linen grave clothes. As the news buzzed through Jerusalem, Peter claimed to have seen Him face to face. Suddenly, as the eleven met to eat and discuss these things, Jesus appeared in their midst. They were terrified, thinking they were seeing a spirit. After considering His wounded hands and feet and observing Him eat a piece of broiled fish and honeycomb, they decided it was He. He was alive! Jesus really had conquered death! He was their resurrected Lord!

It is upon this fact that our faith rises or falls (I Corinthians 15:14). On the basis of God's inspired Word, we must acknowledge the resurrection as a physical, historical event. The *Spirit* bears witness to us today through the resurrection of our Lord Jesus Christ (Romans 8:11). This witness should cause us to reflect upon that momentous event with rejoicing, for it has a powerful implication for our conversion experience. "For if we have been planted together in the likeness of his death, we shall be also in the likeness of his resurrection" (Romans 6:5).

BLOOD

The average adult has five to seven quarts of blood in his body. Twice every minute the heart pumps this vital fluid through the complete network of arteries, veins and capillaries. Every cell of the body is constantly nourished wih oxygen and food. Without this miracle fluid the body would quickly die. Blood disease can have serious consequences, and a blood transfusion can produce amazing results. This physical substance is so closely related to the mystery of life and death that it is no wonder the Lord has used it as a witness of spiritual death and life at conversion.

Blood is common to all humanity. The blood that courses through the veins of every living person on earth is a perpetual witness from God to one aspect of His saving power. Blood is the life fluid of the flesh, carrying food to every cell, fighting disease and eliminating waste. Its delicate chemistry and fascinating function not only speak of God's creative power but also witness to mankind of the shed blood of Jesus Christ.

To God's people, blood holds a very special meaning, invoking feelings of solemnity and awe. It has sacred association with worship. God commanded the Israelites not to use blood for food; blood had to be completely drained from flesh before it could be eaten (Leviticus 19:26). "For the life of the flesh is in the blood: and I have given it to you upon the altar to make an atonement for your souls. . .Therefore, I said unto the children of Israel, ye shall eat the blood of no manner of flesh: for the life of all flesh is the blood thereof" (Leviticus 17:11,14). Even in the New Testament, the Jerusalem Council instructed Gentile Christians to refrain from things strangled and from blood (Acts 15:20).

The Christian emphasis on the blood of Jesus is not the reflection of a primitive blood ritual. God's law still requires blood for the remission of sin. "And almost all things are by the law purged with blood; and without shedding of blood is no remission" (Hebrews 9:22). That blood is required for remission of sin makes it extremely vital to our communion with God. It also magnifies the loving work of our Lord on the cross.

"Forasmuch as ye know that ye were not redeemed with corruptible things, as silver and gold, from your vain conversation received by tradition from your fathers; but with the precious blood of Christ, as of a lamb without blemish and without spot" (I Peter 1:18-19).

The well-known song by Robert Lowery expresses it well:

What can wash away my sin?
Nothing but the blood of Jesus;
What can make me whole again?
Nothing but the blood of Jesus.

Oh! Precious is the flow
That makes me white as snow:
No other fountain I know,
Nothing but the blood of Jesus.

WATER

Water is one of the most common elements in our world. We are reminded of its presence in the air by the clouds that drift overhead as well as by fog, rain, snow and dew. As we view the ocean's vastness and consider the blue area of the globe, we realize there is more water than land. Seven tenths of our earth is covered with water. Not only is there water in the air and on the earth, it is also under the surface of the earth. Some of the most arid spots in the world have found fresh life-sustaining water by tapping into the water table. All of life is sustained by this prevalent liquid. Without water, our verdant world would become a parched lunar wasteland.

Man is dependent upon water in many ways. We pump it into our homes for drinking and cleaning. Farmers use it for irrigation. Water has been used for transportation since the beginning of time. From the days of the old water wheel to the time of the present dynamos it has been a source of power.

"The rain cometh down, and the snow from heaven, and returneth not thither, but watereth the earth, and maketh it bring forth and bud, that it may give seed to the sower, and bread to the eater" *(Isaiah 55:10).*

The availability of water and man's dependence on

21

it for life make it uniquely suited as a witness to salvation. Water is used in the Bible to typify many things. The prophets used water to denote a great multitude of people (Isaiah 8:7; Revelation 17:15). Sometimes water stands for tears (Jeremiah 9:1). At other times it represents children or posterity (Numbers 24:7; Isaiah 48:1). One of the most beautiful uses of water as an example is the comparison of fresh flowing water to the graces and comforts of the Spirit of God. "Ho, every one that thirsteth, come ye to the waters" (Isaiah 55:1). In this book we will deal specifically with water as related to the salvation experience.

First of all, water illustrates trouble and affliction. "Save me, O God; for the waters are come in unto my soul" (Psalm 69:1). Jesus, when speaking of His impending suffering, asked His disciples, "Are ye able to drink of the cup that I shall drink of, and to be baptized with the baptism that I am baptized with?" (Matthew 20:22). Their answer was, "We are able!" They did not realize that He was speaking of His crucifixion, but eventually they did drink of His cup and were baptized with a similar baptism of suffering. All the apostles were martyred except John, and he suffered in many ways for the gospel. All Christians identify with Christ's suffering and death by dying to sin and self-will. "Know ye not, that so many of us as were baptized into Jesus Christ were baptized into his death?" (Romans 6:3). Hence, going to the water with means associating with His suffering.

One of the most obvious uses of water is for washing. Throughout the Bible, water is a cleanser. Not only as a metaphor, but in actual situations it is used repeatedly for the purpose of making things clean. The priests in the Old

Testament washed at the laver of water while performing their religious ritual. Pharoah's daughter came to the Nile River to wash. Jesus took a basin of water and washed the disciples' feet, a practice commonly performed by servants. Jesus sent a blind man to the pool of Siloam to wash his eyes and receive his sight. Many other references also demonstrate the strong association of water with cleansing.

This book will point out how God's witness of water is associated with our salvation. We will show that baptism in water in the name of the Lord Jesus Christ is the witness of water.

Water baptism is compared to the burial of our Lord. We are "buried with Him in baptism" (Colossians 2:12). Baptism in water is the symbolic burial of the carnal man after he has died in repentance. Moreover, according to Scripture, God performs an act of cleansing sins at baptism. In response to the Jews at Jerusalem on the Day of Pentecost, Peter said, "Repent, and be baptized every one of you in the name of Jesus Christ for the remission of sins" (Acts 2:38). Remission means to remove responsibility of, or to pardon. Jesus told His disciples, "Whose soever sins ye remit, they are remitted unto them; and whose soever sins ye retain, they are retained" (John 20:23). Jesus was speaking of the authority vested in the apostles through baptism for the remission or removal of sin.

SPIRIT
There are basically three kinds of spirits in the world: the Holy Spirit and the good angelic spirits, Satan and the evil spirits, and human spirits. *Holy Spirit* is a descriptive title that identifies the manifestation of God's presence.

The spirit of Satan is an evil spirit. Finally, there is the human spirit, which can follow good or evil.

The Human Spirit

Man is composed of spirit, soul, and body (I Thessalonians 5:23). The spirit of man is the eternal aspect of his existence. With the human spirit a person can respond either to the Holy Spirit or to evil spirits. The fundamental response to God should be worship. Also, intuition and communion emanate from the human spirit.

As a study of history reveals, an important characteristic of man is his unending search in the spiritual realm. Man is religious by nature. Atheistic countries in our world are trying to suppress this innate desire of their people, but to no avail. In some cases, man's search has become perverted through astrology, necromancy, witchcraft or overt devil worship.

For the most part, however, people are oblivious to the fact that they have a spiritual nature, because it is suppressed by their carnality. Many people have attended an apostolic church service and commented that they felt something they had never experienced before. Perhaps this was the first time their human spirit had an opportunity to respond to the Spirit of God.

The human spirit is the deepest part of a man. It can be compared to the innermost room of the Tabernacle in the Wilderness.

The Tabernacle was encircled by a fenced yard called the court. The Holy Place was the first and larger room in the Tabernacle building, and there the priests performed their rituals. The inner room, the Holiest of Holies, was most sacred and off-limits to the Israelites and even to the priests.

24

Only the high priest could enter in it, and then only once a year, on the Day of Atonement. The room was dark and isolated. It is like the human spirit, which must be probed for and sought out.

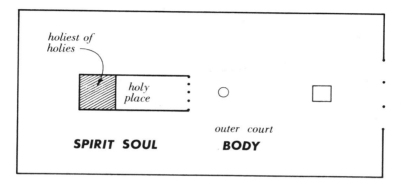

When a person receives salvation, his spirit is brought into communion with God's Spirit. Even though this is a wonderful experience, it is only the beginning of the progressive sychronization of his spirit with God's Spirit. If he will nurture and feed his spirit with prayer, worship and studying the Word of God, his spirit will become the predominant influence on his behavior. In this way he can die to the carnal man and participate in resurrection life of the Lord. "I am crucified with Christ: nevertheless I live; yet not I, but Christ liveth in me" (Galatians 2:20).

God Is a Spirit

The Bible says, "God is a Spirit" (John 4:24). A spirit does not have flesh and bones as we do. The Spirit of God is omnipotent, omnipresent and omniscient. God's Spirit is pure and holy. His Spirit always has been and always will be present. Since we cannot observe God's Spirit through our five senses, we must rely on the human spirit to identify Him.

It is the Spirit of God that initiates any relationship with Himself. Jesus said, "No man can come to me, except the Father which hath sent me draw him" (John 6:44). It is very important to recognize the Spirit of God. For the Christian, God's Spirit is his life source, supplying strength to do things that otherwise would be humanly impossible.

The Spirit of Satan

The spirit of Satan is also very real. This spirit is very deceptive and is diametrically opposed to God's Spirit. Satan's ultimate purpose is to destroy people spiritually and physically and to lead them to eternal destruction. "The thief cometh not, but for to steal, and to kill, and to destroy" (John 10:10). Satan will do anything to arrive at his objective. If he cannot entice a person with beauty, he will try to terrify him with fear. But it is wonderful to have the assurance that God's power is greater than Satan's. With spiritual weapons such as Christ's precious blood, His powerful name, and His appropriated resurrection, we can stand victorious with God's Spirit.

God's Spirit In Us

In the Old Testament, God manifested Himself in a variety of ways: as a man to Abraham, in a burning bush to Moses, through Balaam's donkey, by a pillar of fire and a pillar cloud to the Israelites and in many other ways. These visible manifestations are called theophanies and were only temporary. God's people continually looked forward to a day of greater revelation.

Godly men and women in the Old Testament had a limited knowledge of God. They understood the truth taught by the law of Moses: God holds man guilty for his sins, and man cannot live by God's law without external help. Jesus came to fulfill the law, atone for the sins of mankind, and communicate the glorious attributes of God in a greater measure than the Old Testament had. During Jesus' earthly ministry He healed the sick, cast out devils, spoke words of wisdom, performed miracles and raised the dead. His life was a powerful manifestation of the Spirit of God.

Yet Jesus only ministered to those in His physical presence. He exceeded the greatness of His earthly ministry when He multiplied His Spirit through His church on the Day of Pentecost. This phenomenal outpouring of God's Spirit was not just a historical event; it is a present witness from deity to humanity of the Lord's redemptive work.

"And when the day of Pentecost was fully come, they were all with one accord in one place. And suddenly there came a sound from heaven as of a rushing mighty wind, and it filled all the house where they were sitting. And there appeared unto them cloven tongues like as of fire, and it sat upon each of them. And they were all filled with the Holy Ghost, and began to speak with other tongues, as the Spirit gave them utterance" (Acts 2:1-4).

2.

The Gospel For Us and In Us

TWO ASPECTS OF THE GOSPEL	
work done *for* **us**	**work done** *in* **us**
(*I Cor. 15:1–4*)	(*Acts 2:38*)
1. The Gospel	1. "Fruit" of the Gospel
2. Historical	2. Current
3. Physical	3. Spiritual
4. Complete	4. Progressive
5. Cause	5. Effect
6. Vicarious experience	6. Personal experience
7. Objective	7. Subjective

*T*here are two aspects of the gospel. First, is the work God has done *for* us and, second it is the work He has done *in* us.

The gospel is succinctly defined by the Apostle Paul in I Corinthians 15:1-4. According to this passage of Scripture, the gospel is the *death, burial,* and *resurrection* of Jesus Christ. Although the gospel has many ramifications, these three events define the "gospel in a nutshell."

We should notice first of all that the gospel is the experience of the Lord Jesus Christ. It is historical in nature, recorded in the greatest history book in the world, the Holy Bible. It was a very physical event that involved great physical suffering, real blood, the agony of rejection, and the stark and frightening reality of death. The burial and embalming of the body of Jesus was a very literal event. The resurrection was a miraculous event and yet it is a physical and historical fact.

It is difficult for the human mind to comprehend the magnitude of what Jesus did at Calvary. The God of heaven came to earth, visiting fallen flesh and even becoming one of us, and then He laid down His human life for us. The gospel transcends every event in the annals of human history. No man in history has ever raised himself from the dead—only our Lord Jesus Christ. The work He did is complete. Forever the sin problem has been solved. We cannot add one thing to the perfect and complete work of our

31

Savior. The work of Jesus is so entirely perfect that it is the very substance of the gospel. Our Christian experience is actually the "fruit of the gospel." Regardless of the intensity of our own personal experience, the work of the Lord Jesus Christ surpasses it in magnitude. Without His work for us, we can expect no work to be done in us.

The death, burial and resurrection of Jesus was vicarious in nature. He did not suffer for personal gain, but He suffered that we could have eternal life. The gospel is a beautiful picture of love and compassion. It is not just beautiful rhetoric full of careless promises and romantic nothings. Jesus proved His amazing love by submitting to the executioners when He could have defended Himself. "Greater love hath no man than this, that a man lay down his life for his friends" (John 15:13).

When considering the gospel, we must accept the objective work of the Lord for us. The gospel must be accepted as a historical fact on the basis of God's Word. Even if there is no emotion when we first consider the gospel, we must make a deliberate decision of the will to believe and accept the work of Jesus as a complete work of redemption. This must provide a basis for any experience we receive. Subjective experience that does not stand on the finished work of the Lord Jesus Christ is a spurious experience. Regardless of the religious fervor, it is still subject to the scrutiny of God's Word. On that basis it stands or falls.

The second aspect of the gospel that we need to consider is God's work in us. This initial work of regeneration, which gives us spiritual life, is the fruit of the work of Jesus. Without the redemptive act of our Savior, our experience could just be another sensation.

Everyone has had experiences of a mystical nature—a dream that came true an intuition that turned out to be valid, a sudden feeling of awe and wonder at nature, or a feeling so profound that it defies verbal description. All these unusual experiences are noteworthy, but the greatest of all experiences is the salvation experience. There is no act greater than the death, burial and resurrection of Jesus Christ. Our experience with Jesus Christ in applying and obeying the gospel should not take second place to any other phenomenon in our life.

Our salvation experience should be a reflection of Jesus' experience. Jesus died, we must die. Jesus was buried, we must be buried. Jesus rose from the dead, we must rise from the dead.

The question may arise, "How can this be?" Nicodemus asked the same question in John 3. Jesus told Nicodemus he must be "born again." This ruler misunderstood Jesus to say that when a man is old he must return to his mother's womb. But Jesus was speaking of a spiritual rebirth. "Jesus answered, Verily, verily, I say unto thee, Except a man be born of water and of the Spirit, he cannot enter into the kingdom of God" (John 3:5).

The three aspects of Jesus' experience in the gospel story must be enacted in our experience, in a spiritual way. Our experience is an extension of His. His was historical and physical, ours is present and spiritual.

The three aspects of our obedience to the gospel are clearly defined in Acts 2, which describes the birth of the New Testament church. The 120 disciples of Christ who had been praying and waiting in an upper room in Jerusalem were gloriously filled with the Holy Spirit, accompanied by the initial sign of speaking in other tongues.

Since it was the Day of Pentecost (the fiftieth day after Passover), many Jews from different parts of the world were there. As they began to hear and see this mighty outpouring of God's Spirit, a curious crowd soon gathered.

Peter took advantage of the occasion and began to preach the gospel—the death, burial and resurrection of Jesus Christ (Acts 2:23-24). After he preached the gospel to them, they were pricked in their hearts and asked, "What shall we do?" (They believed the gospel message or they would have never asked this question.) Then Peter told them what to do to obey the gospel.

> *"Then Peter said unto them, Repent, and be baptized every one of you in the name of Jesus Christ for the remission of sins, and ye shall receive the gift of the Holy Ghost" (Acts 2:38).*

This passage identifies the three steps in obeying the gospel: repentance, water baptism, and receiving the Holy Ghost. This message is beautifully confirmed in Romans.

> *"Know ye not, that so many of us as were baptized into Jesus Christ were baptized into his death? Therefore, we are buried with him by baptism into death: that like as Christ was raised up from the dead by the glory of the Father, even so we also should walk in newness of life" (Romans 6:3-4)*

These and other scriptural references explain very explicitly how to obey the gospel. We die with Christ in a spiritual sense by submitting our will to God and by allow-

34

ing the old man (the sinful lifestyle) to die. This is repentance. We are then buried with the Lord by baptism, which is a symbolic burial of the old man after he is dead. We are immersed in water to signify the burial. The name of Jesus Christ is also used as the formula, since we are "buried with him in baptism" (Romans 6:4). The Father was not buried, neither was the Holy Ghost. The Father or the Holy Ghost never died. It was Jesus Christ in the flesh who died. It was also the Lord Jesus Christ who rose again from the dead. If we die with Him by repenting of our sins and if we are buried with Him by baptism, we will rise with Him in newness of life by receiving the baptism of the Holy Ghost.

Our experience in obeying the gospel definitely entails subjective involvement. Repentance is an emotionally moving encounter. It brings sorrow and regret for past rebellion and indifference to God, great peace to the spirit when the death to self is complete. It is a great relief to confess our sins to God and place our lives in His hands. The sweetness of surrender is overwhelming.

Baptism requires physical involvement. We go down into the water to bury the old nature and we experience abundant joy as we realize our sins are remitted. The baptism of the Holy Ghost is the culmination. At that experience, God replaces the death we have died with His life, and we become new creatures. It is more than the bland, unemotional experience some are told to be satisfied with.

"Therefore if any man be in Christ, he is a new creature: old things are passed away; behold, all things are become new" (II Corinthians 5:17).

Our experience in the gospel is not complete at this point, however. The work done *for* us in the Lord Jesus is sufficient and complete, but the work He is doing *in* us is a perpetual work of developing us to maturity. The new birth experience is only the beginning.

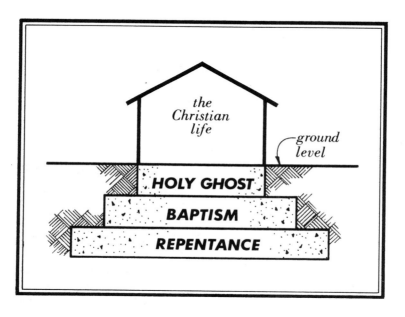

"But grow in grace, and in the knowledge of our Lord and Saviour Jesus Christ" (II Peter 3:18). As important as the initial experience is, it is not the conclusion. It is the foundation upon which a Christian life is built.

3.

The Gospel and God's Witness

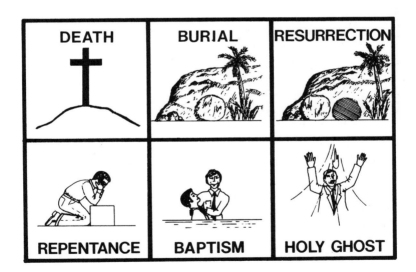

| DEATH | BURIAL | RESURRECTION |
| REPENTANCE | BAPTISM | HOLY GHOST |

BELIEVING AND OBEYING

*T*he word *gospel* literally means the "good news." Matthew, Mark, Luke and John are called the four Gospels because they preserve for us the life and teachings of our Lord Jesus Christ. The gospel in a general sense is the redemptive work of Jesus Christ with all its ramifications. But for our purposes we must ask, "What is the gospel in its simplicity? And how do we obey the gospel?"

Paul defined the gospel in I Corinthians 15:1-4: "Moreover, brethren, I declare unto you the gospel which I preached unto you. . . . For I delivered unto you first of all that which I also received, how that Christ died for our sins according to the scriptures; and that he was buried, and that he rose again the third day according to the scriptures." This passage identifies the death, burial and resurrection of Jesus Christ as the essence of the gospel. These three aspects of the work of Jesus Christ form the bastion of the Christian faith.

Our faith in the death, burial and resurrection of Jesus Christ is vital, but according to the Scriptures, mere mental belief in the gospel is not enough. Christ will be revealed from heaven, "in flaming fire taking vengeance on them that know not God, and that *obey* not the gospel of our Lord Jesus Christ; who shall be punished with everlasting destruction from the presence of the Lord, and from the glory of his power" (II Thessalonians 1:8-9). Those who do not *obey* the gospel will be punished with everlasting destruction. They will be lost and sent to the lake of fire due to their lack of obedience. The gospel demands more from us than just mental assent.

Believe and *obey* have different meanings in modern English. They are not the same. To obey means to comply with or carry out the command or request. A person can *believe* a building is on fire and yet do nothing about it. He can smell the smoke and see the flame. If he does not *obey* his better judgment and get out, however, he will be destroyed in the flame. In the New Testament, genuine faith in Jesus Christ includes obedience to His gospel. Saving faith is not just mental belief; rather, it is obedient faith.

MENTAL BELIEF VERSUS OBEDIENT FAITH

"BELIEVE"	"OBEY"
1. To accept as true	1. To carry out orders
2. Mental assent	2. Physical process
3. Initial approach	3. Resulting action
4. Objective faith	4. Subjective involvement

If the gospel is the death, burial and resurrection of Jesus, how do we obey that gospel? The answer to this question is in the Scriptures. It would be ridiculous to conclude that in order to receive salvation we must physically die on a cross, be buried in a tomb and hope to rise three days later as Jesus did. Rather, obeying the gospel must mean applying or appropriating Christ's work in our lives through a salvation experience that parallels His work in a symbolic way. As shown in Chapter 2, this occurs when we repent of our sins (death), are baptized by immersion in water in the name of Jesus Christ (burial), and receive the Holy Ghost (resurrection).

Let us consider in greater detail these three aspects of our Lord's experience and their application to our life.

DEATH—BLOOD

"And he was clothed with a vesture dipped in blood: and his name is called The Word of God" (Revelation 19:13).

This verse speaks of our Lord's majestic return. Even in His triumphant glory, nothing is more significant than His "vesture dipped in blood." Blood-drenched apparel is linked with His revelation of Himself.

Death by crucifixion is one of the world's most disgraceful and cruel methods of torture. Those who want to discredit the resurrection say that Jesus never really died but only swooned and was placed in a tomb by Joseph of Arimathea. After a few hours they maintain, the coolness of the tomb and the reviving effects of the spices with which He had been embalmed revived Him.

The following points, however, prove beyond any doubt that Jesus really suffered and died:

1. The agony in the garden of Gethsemane. "And being in an agony he prayed more earnestly: and his sweat was as it were great drops of blood falling down to the ground" (Luke 22:44).

2. Betrayal by one of His own disciples and His trial. Jesus was kept awake all night long and taken before An-

41

nas, Caiaphas, the Sanhedrin, Pilate, Herod and finally Pilate again. Throughout these six trials he was slapped, spit upon, buffeted and mocked.

3. The scourging ordered by Pilate, the Roman governor. The Jewish law allowed forty lashes. To avoid violating the law through a mistaken count, the Pharisees only allowed thirty-nine. Jesus was beaten under Roman law, however, which did not require a limit. The following quotation describes a typical Roman scourging:

> *The heavy whip is brought down with full force again and again across shoulders, back and legs. At first the heavy thongs cut through the skin only. Then, as the blows continue, they cut deeper into the subcutaneous tissue, producing first an oozing of blood from the capillarie and veins of the skin, and finally, spurting arterial bleeding from vessels in the underlying muscles. The small balls of lead first produce large, deep bruises which are broken up by subsequent blows. Finally the skin of the back is hanging in long ribbons and the entire area is an unrecognizable mass of torn, bleeding tissue. When it is determined by the centurion in charge that the prisoner is near death, the beating is finally stopped.* [1]

4. The crown of thorns. After placing a crown of thorns on His head, Christ's executioners spit on Him and then beat Him on the head with rods. This drove the sharp points into the skin of His scalp.

5. The crucifixion. The following two quotations describe the ordeal:

The soldiers would feel for the depression at the wrist, then drive the heavy wrought iron spike through at that point. Next, the legs were placed together and a large nail was driven through them. The knees were left moderately flexed, and a seat (known as a "sedecula") was attached to the cross for the buttocks of the victim. [2]

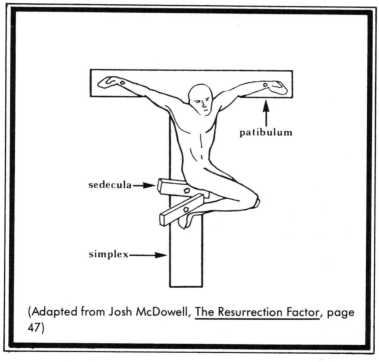

(Adapted from Josh McDowell, The Resurrection Factor, page 47)

As the arms fatigue, great waves of cramps sweep over the muscles, knotting them in deep, relentless, throbbing pain. With these cramps

43

comes the inability to push Himself upward. Hanging by his arms, the pectoral muscles are paralyzed and the intercostal muscles are unable to act. Air can be drawn into the lungs, but cannot be exhaled. Jesus fights to raise Himself in order to get even one short breath. Finally, carbon dioxide builds up in the lungs and in the bloodstream and the cramps partially subside. Spasmodically, He is able to push himself upward to exhale and bring in the life-giving oxygen. [3]

How could Jesus have endured such horrendous suffering and such great loss of blood, then revived Himself, moved the huge stone away from the tomb and walked seven and a half miles from Jerusalem to Emmaus? (Luke 24:13). It would have been impossible; Jesus actually died and then rose again.

The blood shed by Jesus at Calvary represents His human life given up in death. Death to sin and self-will (repentance) cannot be removed from our relationship with Jesus. "Then said Jesus unto his disciples, If any man will come after me, let him deny himself, and take up his cross, and follow me" (Matthew 16:24).

The command to repent is evident in the Scriptures. John the Baptist's message was, "Repent ye: for the kingdom of heaven is at hand" (Matthew 3:2). Among the last words of our Lord were these: "And that repentance and remission of sins should be preached in his name among all nations, beginning at Jerusalem" (Luke 24:47). Paul, preaching at Mars' Hill said, "And the times of this ignorance God winked at; but now commandeth all men every where to repent" (Acts 17:30).

BURIAL—WATER

"Buried with him in baptism" (Colossians 2:12).

The Bible teaches that water baptism identifies us with the burial of Jesus. The following two quotations reveal the importance of water in Jewish burial practices:

> In preparing a body for burial, the Jews would place it on a stone table in the burial chamber. The body first would be washed with warm water. The Babylonian Talmud records that the washing of the body was so important to proper burial, the Jews permitted it even on the Sabbath. [4]

• • •

> The water required for the cleansing of the dead has to be warmed. The ceremonial of washing the corpse must not be performed by one person alone, not even in the case of a child. The dead must likewise not be moved from one position to another by fewer than two persons. The corpse is laid on a board, with its feet turned toward the door, and covered with a clean sheet. . . .The corpse is now washed from head to foot in lukewarm water, during which process the mouth is covered, so that no water should trickle down it.
> While this ceremonial is being carried out, some verses are recited by those who officiate, concluding with the words, "And I will sprinkle clean water upon you and you shall be clean." [5]

How thrilling it is to learn that water was such an important aspect in a Jewish burial. This is another witness to water. As we are immersed in a watery grave, how closely our experience parallels with that of Jesus.

Some assert that baptism is not important, saying, "It is only the outward sign of an inward work." Certainly, the spiritual work of remission of sins is inward, but, does that mean the outward ceremony is not important or necessary? To the contrary, it is part of our obedience to the gospel. The following verses of Scripture indicate the importance of water baptism in the name of Jesus Christ.

1. John 3:5: "Except a man be born of water and of the Spirit, he cannot enter into the kingdom of God."

2. Matthew 3:15: Jesus submitted to baptism to fulfill all righteousness.

3. Matthew 28:19: Among the last words of Jesus to His disciples was the command to baptize.

4. Acts 2:38: Peter's message on the inauguration of the New Testament Church Age, which we are part of, included baptism as necessary.

5. Acts 8:12: Philip baptized the believers at Samaria.

6. Acts 8:38: Philip baptized the Ethiopian eunuch.

7. Acts 9:18; 22:16: Paul was baptized at his conversion.

8. Acts 10:48: Peter commanded Cornelius and his household to be baptized.

9. Acts 16:15: Lydia was baptized when she was converted.

10. Acts 16:33: Paul baptized the Philippian jailer at his conversion at midnight.

11. Acts 19:5: Disciples of John the Baptist were rebaptized when they were converted to Christianity.

12. Romans 6:3-4; Colossians 2:11-12: Baptism is our identification with Christ's burial.

13. Hebrews 6:1-2: "The doctrine of baptisms" is one of the undergirding foundational doctrines.

14. Galatians 3:27: Through baptism we put on Christ.

15. Mark 16:16: "He that believeth and is baptized shall be saved."

16. I Peter 3:21: "The like figure whereunto even baptism doth also now save us."

RESURRECTION—SPIRIT

"And if Christ be not risen, then is our preaching vain, and your faith is also vain" (I Corinthians 15:14).

The Apostle Paul plainly declared the resurrection of Jesus Christ to be the basis of our faith. Without a resurrection our faith is in vain; we are presumptuous and gullible.

Josh McDowell, author of several books giving evidences for the Christian faith, wrote, "The historical fact of the resurrection is the very basis for the truth of Christianity. To put it simply, the resurrection of Jesus Christ and Christianity stand or fall together. One cannot be true without the other."[6]

He further noted that the resurrection of Jesus makes Christianity unique among religions: "All but four of the major world religions are based on mere philosophical propositions. Of the four that are based on personalities rather than a philosophical system, only Christianity claims an empty tomb for its founder."[7] The founders of these other three religions are all dead:

Judaism—Abraham died about 1900 B.C.

Buddhism—Buddha died with no mention of a resurrection.

Islam—Mohammed died June 8, 632 A.D.

The resurrection of Jesus is not just a theological subject. It is a historical fact based upon a host of witnesses. Here is a list of those who witnessed the resurrected Christ:

1. Mary Magdalene (John 20:14; Mark 16:9).

2. Mary Magdalene, Joanna, Mary the mother of James and other women (Luke 24:10; Matthew 28:9-10).

3. Peter (Luke 24:34; I Corinthians 15:5).

4. Two disciples on the road to Emmaus (Luke 24:13-33).

5. The apostles, excluding Thomas (John 20:19-24).

6. The apostles, including Thomas (John 20:26-29).

7. Seven disciples by the Lake of Tiberias (John 21:1-23).

8. More than 500 believers at one time (I Corinthians 15:6).

9. James (I Corinthians 15:7).

10. The eleven apostles (Matthew 28:16-20).

11. The disciples at the ascension (Acts 1:3-12).

12. Paul (I Corinthians 15:8).

13. Stephen (Acts 7:55).

14. John at Patmos (Revelation 1:10-20).

Again we quote Josh McDowell concerning the great variety and number of firsthand witnesses:

Let's take the more than 500 witnesses who saw Jesus alive after His death and burial and place them in a courtroom. Do you realize that if each of these 500 people were to testify only six minutes each, including cross-examination, you would have an amazing 50 hours of firsthand eye-witness testimony? Add to this the testimony of many other eyewitnesses and you could well have the largest and most lopsided trial in history. . . .

Now, something happened. Something happened almost 2,000 years ago that changed the course of history from B.C. (Before Christ) to A.D. (the Latin <u>Anno Domini</u>—the year of our Lord).

That "something" was so dramatic it completely changed all men's lives, so that all but one died a martyr's death.

That something was an empty tomb! An empty tomb that a 15 minute walk from the center of Jerusalem would have confirmed or disproved. [8]

The importance of Christ's resurrection also points to the extreme importance of our spiritual resurrection. The new birth experience, which is essential to salvation, is a life-changing encounter with the risen Christ, who imparts new life by His indwelling Spirit. "Like as Christ was raised up from the dead by the glory of the Father, even so we also should walk in newness of life. For if we have been planted together in the likeness of his death, we shall be also in the likeness of his resurrection" (Romans 6:4-5).

Just as the resurrection is the seal of Jesus' claim to be the Son of God, the baptism of the Holy Spirit is our seal of acceptance as a child of God. "In whom also after that ye believed, ye were sealed with that holy Spirit of promise" (Ephesians 1:13). "And grieve not the holy Spirit of God, whereby ye are sealed unto the day of redemption" (Ephesians 4:30).

The pivotal point of Peter's message on the Day of Pentecost was the resurrection of Jesus Christ (Acts 2:32-36). The very first Christian message used the resurrection to verify the purpose of Jesus' death and to show it as a prophetic fulfillment. Peter confirmed that he and the other apostles were eyewitnesses to the resurrection and stated that the resurrection showed Jesus to be both Lord and Christ. Peter also confirmed that the phenomenon of speaking in tongues was a result of the Lord's resurrection.

At the conclusion of this anointed message, the Jewish gathering asked, "What shall we do?" (Acts 2:37). Then Peter applied the work of Jesus to them directly by instructing them how to appropriate the gospel. "Then Peter said unto them, Repent, and be baptized every one of you in the name of Jesus Christ for the remission of sins, and ye shall receive the gift of the Holy Ghost" (Acts 2:38).

Three thousand souls responded to Peter's message that day. The streets of Jerusalem must have been filled with excitement when these newborn converts dispersed throughout the city proclaiming the joy of their new birth experience.

The revival did not end at Pentecost. In Acts 4 five thousand more were converted. This began a rapid and continued growth for the Christian church. Miracles and signs accompanied the believers as they proclaimed their resurrected Lord.

This great beginning can be viewed with cold intellectual observation as mere historical fact, as a bygone event of time and space. We can read the miraculous account of the Acts of the Apostles with a nod of approval, not realizing its application to the present. Our responsibility as Christians, however, is not just to preserve history but to display before the world the living Christ. "Jesus Christ the same yesterday, and to day, and for ever" (Hebrews 13:8).

To minimize the importance of the baptism of the Holy Spirit is to minimize our resurrection with Jesus Christ. Mentally believing in the resurrection as part of the gospel is not the same as obeying. When we truly have saving faith in the gospel, we will obey and receive the Holy Ghost. "Now if any man have not the Spirit of Christ, he is none of his" (Romans 8:9).

FOOTNOTES

[1]C. Truman Davis, "The Crucifixion of Jesus," *Arizona Medicine,* March 1965, p. 185.

[2]Josh McDowell, *The Resurrection Factor,* (San Bernardino: Here's Life Publishers, 1981), p. 46.

[3]Davis, "The Crucifixion of Jesus," p. 186.

[4]McDowell, *Resurrection,* p. 51.

[5]A. P. Bender, "Beliefs, Rites, and Customs of the Jews, Connected with Death, Burial and Mourning," *The Jewish Quarterly Review,* Vol. VII (1895), pp. 250-260.

[6]McDowell, *Resurrection,* p. 14.

[7]McDowell, *Evidence that Demands a Verdict,* (San Bernardino: Campus Crusade for Christ, 1972), p. 186.

[8]McDowell, *Resurrection,* pp. 64, 72.

4.

The Passover As God's Witness

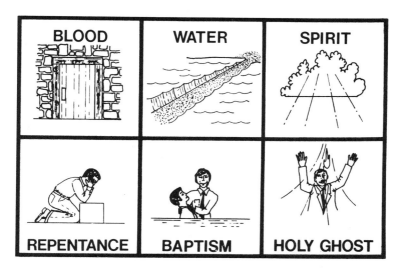

"*Moreover, brethren, I would not that ye should be ignorant, how that all our fathers were under the cloud, and all passed through the sea; and were all baptized unto Moses in the cloud and in the sea*" (I Corinthians 10:1-2).

*T*he deliverance God gave to the Israelites from Egypt is a type of our transition from sin into the kingdom of God. This great deliverance is still celebrated by the Jews today by a festival called Pesach or Passover. This commemoration has been perpetuated through the years as a witness to the delivering power of God. Just as God delivered Israel from the death angel almost 3500 years ago, He delivers sinners today from eternal death.

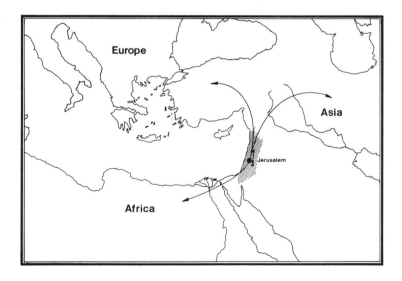

God promised Abraham that the land of Canaan was given to him and his seed (Genesis 12:6-7). It was God's intention to plant these people, who were believers in one God, on the land bridge of the world.

He wanted His chosen people to be on display to the rest of the world as a witness of the one true God. And this was to be accomplished by locating them in this well-travelled area.

God warned Abraham, however, that his descendants would sojourn in a strange land and be afflicted for 400 years before they acquired Canaan permanently (Genesis 15:13). This sojourn began when Joseph was sold into slavery by his brothers to a Midianite caravan who in turn sold him as a slave to Potiphar in Egypt. Joseph was blessed of God and had the ability to make the best of every unpleasant situation. He rose in rank from a slave to a ruler in Egypt in spite of many adverse trials.

During seven years of famine, Jacob sent his sons to Egypt to buy grain. Joseph's brothers stood before him and begged for help not knowing his identity. After Joseph disclosed himself as their brother, he sent them to get his father Jacob.

Joseph provided for the seventy members of his family in the land of Goshen. They increased and multiplied in this rich fertile land under the protection of the kingdom of Egypt.

> *"And the children of Israel were fruitful, and increased abundantly, and multiplied, and waxed exceeding mighty; and the land was filled with them" (Exodus 1:7).*

After the death of Joseph, there arose an Egyptian monarch who had not known Joseph. The Israelites were stripped of all their rights and reduced to common slaves. They were put under taskmasters and required to make bricks. The more Pharoah afflicted the Israelites, the more they multiplied. He initiated stronger measures of oppression by demanding that all newborn male children be thrown into the river. During this time, Moses was born. He was to be God's instrument of deliverance from this great oppression.

Through some very unusual circumstances, Moses was adopted by Pharoah's daughter and was nursed by his own mother. After forty years in Pharaoh's court, Moses murdered an Egyptian and fled to the wilderness to escape the wrath of Pharaoh. There he lived for another forty years.

While in the wilderness, God called Moses to lead Israel out of this horrible bondage and gave him miraculous signs to confirm his calling. Through a burning bush, God spoke to Moses of the great deliverance he would bring to Israel.

> *"And the LORD said, I have surely seen the affliction of my people which are in Egypt, and have heard their cry by reason of their taskmasters; for I know their sorrows: and I am come down to deliver them out of the hand of the Egyptians, and to bring them up out of that land unto a good land and a large, unto a land flowing with milk and honey" (Exodus 3:7-8).*

Just as the Israelites were in bondage and afflicted by Egyptian taskmasters, so is the human race incarcerated in a spiritual bondage. Sin enslaves and afflicts mankind. Satan wants to destroy our family, health and peace of mind and, most of all, he wants to destroy us spiritually. Men and women today are frantically searching for something to relieve the pressure of life's problems. Unfortunately, so many are seeking answers through carnal things, but there is no answer to man's dilemma in the carnal realm. This world can only offer substitutes for true deliverance. The only answer is to be reborn spiritually, to rise up and move out of the carnal world into a spiritual world

God gave Moses special power and authority to lead the Israelites out of their bondage in Egypt. For 430 years they had lived in this land. Now God was moving them out.

Moses and Aaron, his brother, went to Pharaoh and asked that the Israelites be allowed to go to the wilderness to worship their God. Pharoah mocked them. "And Pharaoh said, Who is the LORD, that I should obey his voice to let Israel go? I know not the LORD, neither will I let Israel go" (Exodus 5:2). Pharaoh reminded them they were his slaves and demanded that they return to their burdens. He then afflicted them even more, requiring them to make the same number of bricks as before and yet gather their own straw and stubble.

Pharaoh's rebellion caused, a series of plagues to come upon the Egyptians. First of all, God turned the water to blood. Then He caused frogs to cover the land. Dust became lice upon man and beast. Flies covered the land. The cattle began to die from a terrible plague. Men and beasts broke out with boils. The Lord then sent thunder, hail and fire. The vegetation that remained after the fire and hail was eaten by swarms of locusts. Moses then stretched forth his hand toward heaven and darkness covered the land for three days. After each plague, Moses entreated Pharaoh to let Israel go. Each time Pharaoh refused.

Prior to the tenth and final plague, God gave Moses instructions for Israel to prepare to leave the land of Egypt. After this plague the Israelites received deliverance from Egyptian bondage, and involved in their deliverance were three elements or witnesses: blood, water and Spirit. Their deliverance from Egypt is a type of our deliverance from sin into the kingdom of God, and the same three elements figure prominently as a witness to our salvation today.

BLOOD

The tenth and final plague upon Egypt was the death of the firstborn in every family. It was the most severe of all the plagues. This was God's crushing blow upon Pharaoh's rebellion.

God warned the Israelites that the death angel would enter every home throughout Egypt. Even the Israelite families would suffer loss unless they met certain requirements. God had protected Israel from other plagues without any effort on their part, but this time He required active obedience in order for them to escape the great, final plague.

In a similar manner, the Lord today blesses many people who do not exert much effort to serve God. The Lord blesses their faith even though it may be small. There comes a time, however, when every person must totally commit himself to God in obedient faith in order to be saved. Complete deliverance means more than just being blessed of God and remaining in Egypt. To get out of Egypt, a price must be paid. The price is blood (death).

Blood had to be shed in every home in the Israelite

community in order for it to be spared the destruction of the death angel. God instructed Moses that every family was to select a lamb without any blemish. It was to be a male of the first year. Goats were also acceptable. The Israelites were to select the lamb on the tenth day of the month and keep it up until the fourteenth day. On the fourteenth day, the sacrifice was to be killed in the evening and roasted over a fire. After the lamb was roasted they were to eat the meat with their loins girded, their shoes on their feet, and their staffs in their hands. God wanted them in a mobile position. They were on the verge of moving out of bondage; the Lord was about to move them to a better place.

Along with this Passover supper, they ate bitter herbs and unleavened bread. This supper is a type of our self-denial and repentance when leaving the old life of sin. Repentance is bitter and unpleasant until we pass the initial point of decision. Then it becomes a glorious, cleansing experience. There is a sweetness in surrendering to God without reservation.

In Israel's deliverance, blood had great significance. When the sacrifice was slain, the blood was caught in a basin. God instructed them to take some hyssop, dip it in the basin of blood and sprinkle it on the lintel and the two side posts of the house in which the sacrifice was eaten. The blood upon the door was to be a token or a witness to Israel.

Perhaps not understanding why all this ritual was necessary, the Israelites were obedient nevertheless. The blood was the sign or witness to the death angel that he was not to enter. The blood was like a protective envelopment over each house; it preserved the occupants from the final plague.

"For I will pass through the land of Egypt this night, and will smite all the firstborn in the land of Egypt, both man and beast; and against all the gods of Egypt I will execute judgment: I am the LORD. And the blood shall be to you for a token upon the houses where ye are: and when I see the blood, I will pass over you, and the plague shall not be upon you to destroy you, when I smite the land of Egypt" (Exodus 12:12-13).

The death of the lamb and the application of blood in Israel's deliverance is a type of the death of Christ and also of our repentance. Our turn from sin to God and our repentant life style is described in Scripture as a death to sin and a crucifixion of the sinful self (Romans 6:2, 6; Galatians 5:24; 6:14; I Peter 2:24). Jesus said, "Except ye repent, ye shall all likewise perish" (Luke 13:3). Repentance is the witness of blood. It is a death to self and the means whereby we appropriate the power of the precious blood of Jesus to turn away from sin.

REPENTANCE

Repentance is first of all a decision of the will. It is a person's firm decision to change his way of thinking to conform to God's way. It is a change of his behavior, making the Lord Jesus truly his Lord. Repentance is not just mental belief in the gospel, but it is action, moving toward full obedience.

The second aspect of repentance is the pang of sorrow for past sins. There is a feeling of regret as the repentant person considers his sinful past—regret for the way he has hurt himself as well as for his negative influence upon others. Most of all, he feels saddened when considering how he has ignored the Lord's sacrifice, love and divine will. Christ gave His life for everyone, and the sinner has given nothing in return.

"For godly sorrow worketh repentance to salvation not to be repented of: but the sorrow of the world worketh death" (II Corinthians 7:10). Godly sorrow is not self-pity. It is humility and self-abasement. It is realizing our utter dependence upon the Lord Jesus to rescue us from total destruction of body and spirit. Repentance is recognizing and confessing the sinfulness of man and acknowledging the sovereignty of God.

Due to the abasement of self and the crucifixion of the old nature, it is obvious why repentance is compared to bloodshed and death. Just as the Israelites killed the paschal lamb and applied the blood to the door of their dwelling, so must we die a spiritual death so that the blood of the Lamb of God slain from the foundation of the world can be applied to the door of our hearts.

"Repent ye therefore, and be converted, that your sins may be blotted out, when the times of refreshing shall come from the presence of the Lord" (Acts 3:19).

WATER

The dreadful tenth plague broke the impasse between Israel and Egypt. Pharaoh rose up in the night and discovered his firstborn was dead, for the Lord had killed all the firstborn in the land, man and beast (Exodus 12:29). All of Egypt began to cry and bemoan this traumatic calamity. While it was still night, Pharaoh called Moses and Aaron and demanded they get out of the land and take all their possessions with them.

The Israelite men, women, children and cattle began their departure before it was yet day. This stream of humanity and possessions advanced enthusiastically toward a "land flowing with milk and honey." It has been estimated there were as many as two or three million people in this mass. They turned their backs permanently on 430 years of sojourn in a strange country. Their long-awaited deliverance had finally arrived. This was an exciting and eventful occasion to be commemorated for years to come.

The sacrifice had been slain, the blood had been shed, the Passover meal was completed, the death angel had passed over their dwellings and Pharaoh had officially given them leave. The Israelites did not realize, however, that God had another witness before their final separation. They had already experienced the witness of blood. Next they were to experience the witness of water.

God deliberately allowed them to confront an impossible situation. They came to the banks of the Red Sea and faced a formidable natural barrier. Pharaoh saw what he considered a choice moment to overtake Israel. He decided he could not do without his slave labor force. Preparing 600 chosen chariots and all the chariots of Egypt, Pharaoh pursued after his escaping slaves.

When Israel saw the dust of chariot wheels behind them and the Red Sea before them, they felt trapped. It *was* a trap—not for Israel, but for Pharaoh's army. Impossible situations in the lives of God's people are only opportunities for God to show His delivering power. Satan can be trapped by his own efforts to ensnare the righteous. "Surely he shall deliver thee from the snare of the fowler" (Psalm 91:3).

The Israelites trembled as they considered the water before them. It was seemingly a barrier to their escape. In despair, they cried out to the Lord and to Moses. They could see themselves and their children being run down by Pharaoh's chariots. They did not realize that the very water which appeared to be their obstruction would become the means of their separation from Egypt and the means of the destruction of Pharaoh's army.

Moses quieted the people, urging them to believe the Lord for deliverance. God put a cloud of darkness between the Egyptians and the Israelites. While the Egyptians were in darkness, the Israelites had light.

> *"And Moses stretched out his hand over the sea; and the LORD caused the sea to go back by a strong east wind all that night, and made the sea dry land, and the waters were divided" (Exodus 14:21).*

With a transparent dam on either side of them, the Israelites marched across on dry ground. They passed through the water, but their clothes did not even get damp. Throughout the night they traversed to the other side through God's special escape route. By morning, they were amassed safely on the other side.

Immediately, Pharaoh's army began crossing over also. As the Israelites stood on the bank of the Red Sea watching the approaching chariots in horror, they witnessed another miracle. Their enemy's chariot wheels began to fall off, creating a traffic jam between the two walls of water. Suddenly the two invisible dams broke. Water rushed toward the Egyptians like two giant tidal waves, engulfing them in a massive spray of water and foam. So devastating was the force of the water that not one man escaped.

As the churning water began to rest, the Israelites began to find bodies of the dead Egyptians along the shore. Then Moses and the Israelites began to sing a song of victory and worship to God for His miraculous deliverance. Miriam, Moses' sister, led the women in dances. The timbrel became an instrument of worship in Miriam's hands. All of Israel rejoiced. What a great day this was for these freshly escaped slaves. Now they were securely separated from their enemies. No longer were they subject to a tyrant king. The taskmaster's whip would no longer be their tormentor.

The crossing of the Red Sea was God's witness of water. Just as the blood on the doorpost is a type of repentance in our conversion experience, the crossing of the Red Sea is a type of our water baptism.

I Corinthians 10:1-2 describes the crossing of the sea as a type of our baptism experience. Just as Israel's passing through the waters of the Red Sea gave them deliverance from Pharaoh's army and separated them from Egypt, so our passage through the waters of baptism is a part of our deliverance from the old life of sin and bondage.

When comparing Israel's crossing of the Red Sea with our baptism experience, the following points are noteworthy.

1. *Israel was not officially separated from Egypt until they were safely across the Red Sea.* We are not completely separated from our old life until we have been baptized by immersion in the name of Jesus Christ. Not only are we baptized to follow the example of the New Testament church, but water baptism is part of the new birth

experience. Jesus said, "Except a man be born of water and of the Spirit, he cannot enter into the kingdom of God" (John 3:5).

Baptism is a physical demonstration of the spiritual burial of the old man, the old life. The water itself is not sacred. The ritual of baptism is not a supreme act to be hallowed as a saving act in itself. Nevertheless, God has chosen to permanently separate a person from his sins at baptism (Acts 2:38; 22:16). The significant thing at baptism is obedience to God, submission to God's instructions.

An understanding and appreciation of baptism's meaning is important. Prior repentance and faith is necessary. When a person obeys God's command to be baptized, his baptism becomes the point of separation from his old life as he moves into new life. "He that believeth and is baptized shall be saved; but he that believeth not shall be damned" (Mark 16:16).

2. *Israel's enemies were destroyed by the Red Sea.* The Egyptians were not to be Israel's only enemies, but they were the barrier preventing initial escape to freedom. They were the most imposing enemy. When we are baptized, our most imposing enemy is buried. The old man that died in repentance is buried in baptism. Through baptism in water we are free from the sins of the past.

Acts 2:38 commands, "Be baptized every one of you in the name of Jesus Christ for the remission of sins." Remission means complete pardon and forgiveness. Luke's account of the Great Commission says, "And that repentance and remission of sins should be preached in his name among all nations, beginning at Jerusalem," speaking of baptism as the point where our sins are eradicated, never to be remembered again (Luke 24:47).

Jesus told His disciples, "Whose soever sins ye remit, they are remitted unto them; and whose soever sins ye retain, they are retained" (John 20:23). Of course, the disciples did not have power to forgive sin. Only God can forgive or remit sin (Mark 2:7). But the disciples did baptize believers in the name of Jesus Christ, and thereby their converts received remission of sins.

3. *After crossing over the Red Sea, the Israelites were at a place of total dependence upon God.* They were at a point of no return. After a person has repented and been baptized, he is at a point of no return. He is ready to give up his independence and to accept a life of total dependence upon God. He is then ready to look to God for guidance and sustenance. Peter at Pentecost declared that after a person has repented and been baptized he "shall receive the gift of the Holy Ghost" (Acts 2:38).

"For as many of you as have been baptized into Christ have put on Christ" (Galatians 3:27). By baptism of water and Spirit we "put on" Christ. At baptism the water becomes a witness to the repentant person. Then he is ready for the witness of the Spirit.

SPIRIT

"And the LORD went before them by day in a pillar of a cloud, to lead them the way; and by night in a pillar of fire, to give them light; to go by day and night: He took not away the pillar of the cloud by day, nor the pillar of fire by night, from before the people" (Exodus 13:21-22).

We have seen how Israel received a witness of blood

and of water in their deliverance from Egyptian bondage. Now let us consider the witness of the Spirit.

Once Israel was safely out of Egypt, it might be assumed they would not need any further assistance from God. But they were not weaned from dependence upon the Miracle Worker. They needed God more than ever. How were they to find enough food and water for a caravan of over two million people plus cattle? How would a mass of men, women and children, who knew nothing about warfare, defend themselves against inevitable enemies? How would they survive in the hot, dry Sinai Wilderness? How could such a crowd be organized for survival?

They were out of Egypt but not out of trouble. They needed God's supernatural intervention in a greater way than ever before. The help they needed now was not just a one-time fix for a temporary problem. They needed God's consistent help. Daily miracles were necessary now.

God brought them out of Egypt to bring them into the land of Canaan. He had given them a witness of blood and of water to His delivering power, but He would not leave them now. He manifested Himself to them perpetually by the witness of the Spirit.

One of God's outstanding aids to Israel was a pillar of a cloud by day and a pillar of fire by night. The cloud sheltered them from the blistering desert sun and provided built-in air conditioning for their comfort. A desert becomes very cold at night, and the pillar of fire at night reduced the chill. It also provided street lighting to make their camping safe from the perils of darkness.

The primary purpose of the cloud and fire was the provision of divine guidance. When the cloud or fire moved, Israel moved. This movement was an obvious sign to the entire camp of God's desire to be their guide. God wanted to take them to a "land flowing with milk and honey." Just getting them out of Egypt was not God's total objective. He wanted to take them to a land of their own so they could enjoy a love relationship with their God.

The cloud and fire were not God's only means of protection and provision for Israel. He always provided water for them, even out of a rock when necessary. He fed them with manna and quail. Their clothing never wore out. They had the provision of good health. But the cloud and fire were constant companions of Israel, nurturing them along their way and providing an ever-present witness of God's Spirit.

According to I Corinthians 10:1-2, this witness of the Spirit is a type of the baptism of the Holy Ghost, which a person receives when he is converted and delivered from spiritual bondage. This is the same experience received by the Early Church in Acts 2 with the evidence of speaking with other tongues as the Spirit gave the utterance. In the following ways, our witness of the Spirit parallels Israel's witness of the pillar of cloud and pillar of fire.

1. *The cloud was a comfort from the burning desert sun and the fire was a protection from the chill of the cold nights.* Jesus called the Holy Spirit the Comforter and promised that the Comforter would come to His disciples (John 14:16, 26; 15:26; 16:7). The Lord knew that a person who decides to serve Him will need comfort and assistance, for every human on the earth has problems. The Holy Spirit is sent to all believers to aid and comfort them in their darkest trials. Those who are not Christians must face life's disappointments alone, but we have the comfort of the Lord through the Holy Ghost.

All of the Israelites who stayed under the shadow of the cloud were sheltered, but if they exposed themselves to the sun excessively they would have heat strokes, their skin would blister, and their bodies would dehydrate. Some have received the Holy Spirit but do not enjoy the full benefits of their inheritance. They have wandered from their provision. The problem is not the insufficiency of the Holy Spirit, but their disobedience.

Isaiah prophesied about this experience: "This is the rest wherewith ye may cause the weary to rest; and this is the refreshing" (Isaiah 28:12). Jesus told the woman at the well that those who drank of the water He would give would never thirst again (John 4:14). Jesus was speaking specifically about the Holy Spirit when He said, "Out of his belly shall flow rivers of living water" (John 7:38-39).

2. *The cloud and the fire both provided divine direction and the pillar of fire by night provided light.* This is a type of the Holy Spirit in that the Spirit brings guidance and illumination to our understanding. The baptism of the Holy Ghost gives a person an understanding of God's Word and of life that otherwise he would not have. Jesus said the Holy Spirit "shall teach you all things" (John 14:26). Also, John 16:13 says, "Howbeit when he, the Spirit of truth, is come, he will guide you into all truth."

5.

The Tabernacle As God's Witness

BLOOD	WATER	SPIRIT
REPENTANCE	BAPTISM	HOLY GHOST

"The Holy Ghost this signifying, that the way into the holiest of all was not yet made manifest, while as the first tabernacle was yet standing: which was a figure for the time then present, in which were offered both gifts and sacrifices, that could not make him that did the service perfect. . . .But Christ being come an high priest of good things to come, by a greater and more perfect tabernacle, not made with hands, that is to say, not of this building" (Hebrews 9:8-9, 11).

71

*A*ccording to Hebrews 9, the Tabernacle of the Old Testament is a type of New Testament salvation. A Bible scholar has written this description of the Tabernacle:

> *Imagine a fifteen-by-forty-five-foot house, constructed of three tons of gold, five tons of silver, four tons of brass, and an assortment of jewels, fine wood, and fancy tapestries. This was the tabernacle, the portable house of worship built by a horde of escaped slaves. In the providence of God, the amazing project was financed by the farewell gifts to the children of Israel by their erstwhile captors, the Egyptians. Considering labor and materials prescribed by God Himself, such a building could not be erected today for less than $10 million.* [1]

The Tabernacle was God's method of communing and dwelling with Israel. "And let them make me a sanctuary; that I may dwell among them" (Exodus 25:8). This portable tentlike structure was to be a place of worship and sacrifice. Its exact specifications were given to Moses at Mt. Sinai (Exodus 25-31).

Since the Israelites were a mobile people, this tent sanctuary became God's localized dwelling place in Israel for 400 years. Even after reaching Canaan, the Tabernacle

73

was erected at Shiloh. It was not until Solomon's Temple was constructed that the Tabernacle was no longer used.

Although the Tabernacle had an immediate use for the Israelites, it also became a type or shadow of something better to come. The law of Moses, of which the Tabernacle was a part, is described as a "schoolmaster" to bring us to Christ (Galatians 3:24). The entire Tabernacle plan, priesthood and ceremonial law is rich with typology relating to the work of Jesus Christ and illustrates man's approach to God. A step-by-step analysis of the priest's approach to God in the Tabernacle reveals important corresponding truths concerning our approach to God today.

The innermost room of the Tabernacle was called the Holiest of Holies. This room is a type of heaven and of the abiding presence of God's Holy Spirit. "For Christ is not entered into the holy places made with hands, which are the figures of the true; but into heaven itself, now to appear in the presence of God for us" (Hebrews 9:24). It is a type of heaven in the following ways.

1. *Only the high priest could enter the Holiest of Holies.* In the New Testament church, every believer is a priest and Jesus Christ is the high priest (Hebrews 4:14; I Peter 2:9). Only the high priest could enter into the Holiest of Holies and then only once a year, on the Day of Atonement. Jesus Christ our high priest is the only one who has gone to heaven. "We have such an high priest, who is set on the right hand of the throne of the Majesty in the heavens; a minister of the sanctuary, and of the true tabernacle, which the Lord pitched, and not man" (Hebrews 8:1-2).

2. *The room was a fifteen-foot cube.* The holy city described in Revelation 21:16 is a perfect cube.

3. *It was the epitome of holiness and sanctity.* This room was the most sacred spot on the face of the earth. Heaven is a perfect and holy place. The priest had to be pure before entering the Holiest of Holies. Purity is also required to enter heaven. The mercy seat had a cherub at each end. Heaven is the home of angels.

4. *It was God's dwelling place on earth and the place where He judged sin.* The high priest, on the Day of Atonement, stepped behind the veil and sprinkled blood on the mercy seat (the lid of the ark of the covenant in the Holiest of Holies). The wrath of God would descend to punish Israel's sins, but, upon touching innocent blood, his wrath would turn to mercy. The "throne of his glory" will be the Lord's place of judgment in the end (Matthew 25:31).

5. *It had a veil of separation.* The partition between the Holy Place and the Holiest of Holies was a veil of heavy linen. At the death of Jesus the veil was rent from top to bottom, allowing access into the presence of God. The torn veil symbolizes death or passage from this life into the next.

The Tabernacle illustrates man's approach to God and his journey to heaven. It shows us the New Testament salvation plan step by step.

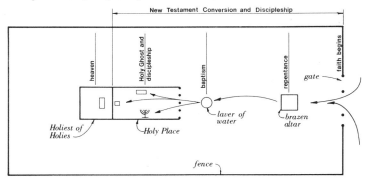

FAITH IN THE GOSPEL

Our faith in the gospel is beautifully illustrated by the Tabernacle plan.

The Tabernacle was surrounded by a seven-and-a-half-foot-high white linen fence. On the east side of the Tabernacle was a thirty foot entrance. This entrance was made of blue, purple, scarlet and white linen curtains supported by four wooden pillars that were covered with silver and set in bases of brass.

Faith is the basis of our coming to God for salvation. Passing through this entrance is a type of our initial leap of faith. Here are some additional illustrations that can be gleaned from the Tabernacle plan.

1. *As the four posts supported the entrance curtains, so the gospel message supports our faith.* Matthew, Mark, Luke and John relate the gospel story of Christ's death, burial and resurrection. Our faith rests upon and comes by the Word of God (Romans 10:17).

2. *The curtains were of four colors* that signify important truths about Jesus. Jesus said, "I am the door: by me if any man enter in, he shall be saved" (John 10:9). Entering into the door of faith in Jesus Christ necessitates acceptance of all the things God's Word says about Him. Four outstanding virtues are typified by the colored curtains. For a person to be prepared to receive the salvation experience he must believe the following things about the Lord Jesus Christ as typified in the colored curtains.

Blue curtain. Blue speaks of Christ's heavenly nature. Jesus was not just a man. He was "God. . .manifest in the flesh" (I Timothy 3:16). The Word who in the beginning was with God and was God "was made flesh and dwelt

76

among us" (John 1:1, 14).

Purple Curtain. Purple was the ancient color of royalty. Jesus was the King of the Jews. His lineage can be traced back to King David. The Jewish nation as a whole rejected their king, but some accepted Him, and "as many as received him, to them gave he power to become the sons of God" (John 1:12). To be saved a person must accept Him as king of this life now as well as accepting Him as king for eternity.

Scarlet Curtain. Scarlet represents the humanity of Jesus and His atoning sacrifice. Jesus was tempted of Satan in the wilderness, became weary, expressed righteous anger, and shed real human blood at Calvary. To be saved a person must put trust in the cleansing blood of the Lord Jesus Christ. "In whom we have redemption through his blood" (Ephesians 1:7).

White Curtain. White is symbolic of the Lord's sinlessness. He was tempted in all points as we are yet com-

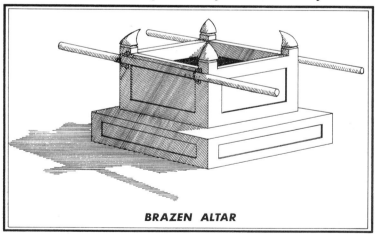

BRAZEN ALTAR

mitted no sin (Hebrews 4:15). Only by the Lord's righteousness are we saved, not by self-righteousness.

BLOOD: BRAZEN ALTAR

The first piece of furniture someone encountered upon entering into the Tabernacle courtyard was the brazen altar. It was seven and one half feet square and four and one half feet high. It was constructed from acacia wood overlaid with brass. A brass horn was mounted at each corner. Inside the altar and halfway down was a grate to hold the sacrifice. At the four corners were rings to hold poles to be used in carrying the alter. These poles were made of acacia wood covered with brass. The altar was hollow inside and was filled with earth. A ledge was built about halfway up the side and went around the altar to provide a place for the priest to stand and minister.

The altar was a witness of blood. Various kinds of offerings were offered upon the brazen altar. Although some offerings required grain or flour cakes, the majority were animal sacrifices. The sacrificer would select an animal free of defects and bring it to the Tabernacle. He would place his hands upon its head while stating the reason for the sacrifice. This was a symbolic transfer of sin to the animal. The animal was then killed in a violent way upon the brazen altar. The blood was sprinkled upon the altar, thrown against the sides, or poured out at the altar's base, depending upon the type of sacrifice being made. After the blood was applied, some portions of the offering could be eaten while other parts were burned on the altar. One writer has estimated the number of blood sacrifices offered:

Official public sacrifices prescribed by law would number altogether 1,273 a year (Numbers 28:1-29:39). If regularly observed, this would amount to almost 2,000,000 from Moses to Christ, apart from the countless millions of unnumbered individual offerings and additional public sacrifices. [2]

At the end of a typical day around the brazen altar, blood would be everywhere. The priest's garments would be splotched with blood and the earth would be saturated with standing pools of blood. The brazen altar must have been smeared and splattered with blood by the countless sacrifices offered. The entire scene was a macabre exhibition of blood and death.

These blood sacrifices were a foreshadowing of the perfect Lamb as sacrifice to come (Hebrews 10). Every animal offered on the brazen altar was a type of Jesus Christ's death at Calvary. But the Lord was the only perfect sacrifice; only His blood forever cleanses from sin. "But this man, after he had offered one sacrifice for sins for ever, sat down on the right hand of God" (Hebrews 10:12).

As a type of Jesus' death, the altar is also a beautiful type of our death with Him in repentance. The following points show how the brazen altar is symbolic of our death with the Lord Jesus Christ.

1. *The prominence of the brazen altar.* It was the first piece of furniture in the Tabernacle courtyard. It was large and imposing. When a person approached the Holy Place, it stood directly in front of him. It was unavoidable!

When a person begins to believe the gospel, the first step of obedience is repentance. He can get no further with

God until he dies out to the old man. Humility in approaching God is an eternal principle of God's Word. In His dealings with Israel He said, "If my people, which are called by my name, shall humble themselves, and pray, and seek my face, and turn from their wicked ways; then will I hear from heaven, and will forgive their sin, and will heal their land" (II Chronicles 7:14). That is repentance, and it is necessary in order to enter into fellowship with God. "And the times of this ignorance God winked at; but now commandeth all men every where to repent" (Acts 17:30).

2. *The brass construction.* The altar and the poles for carrying it were made of wood covered with brass. Also, the ash buckets, shovels, basins, carcass-hooks and fire pans were all of brass. During this time, weapons of war were made of brass, and brass in the Bible indicates judgment. (See Revelation 1:15, 2:18.) How appropriate it was that the altar be brass, for there God judged sin.

There is no exception to God's judgment of sin. "For the wages of sin is death" (Romans 6:23). After sin was symbolically transferred to the sacrificial animal by the laying on of hands, the animal was killed to satisfy God's judgment until the true Sacrifice came. Jesus took upon Himself the sins of the whole world and died, ultimately bearing the divine judgment for all sinners.

> *"And they that are Christ's have crucified the flesh with the affections and lusts" (Galatians 5:24).*
>
> *"God forbid that I should glory, save in the cross of our Lord Jesus Christ, by whom the world is crucified unto me, and I unto the world" (Galatians 6:14).*

When a person repents, he is crucified with Christ. This begins his identification with Christ's atoning death, burial and resurrection, which takes away sin.

At repentance, a person's sins are judged as he rests his faith in the blood of Jesus. Repentance, coupled with water baptism, passes the judgment to the redemptive work of the Lord Jesus, and we receive this promise: "Some men's sins are open beforehand, going before to judgment" (I Timothy 5:24).

3. *The horns of the altar.* The horns were used to bind the sacrifice to the altar. "Bind the sacrifice with cords, even unto the horns of the altar" (Psalm 118:27). Jesus made a deliberate and thoughtful decision to die on the cross. He actually made the final commitment in the Garden of Gethsemane when He prayed in great agony and sorrow, "Not my will, but thine, be done" (Luke 22:42). It was not the nails that held Jesus to the cross but His resolute decision, motivated by love. The sacrifice Jesus offered up at Calvary was securely bound to the altar with cords of love.

Our decision in repentance should be steadfast and solid like that of Jesus. By tying our sacrifice down with a strong decision, we will prevent the old man from reviving and retreating from the life of discipleship. Repentance is not just an initial experience but a recurrent commitment as we grow in the Lord. And our commitment to Jesus should be a reciprocating bond of love.

4. *The continual fire.* "The fire shall ever be burning upon the altar; it shall never go out" (Leviticus 6:13). Fire is also symbolic of judgment. (See Matthew 3:11-12; I Corinthians 3:13-15). That the fire never was to be put out is good news for it signifies that the Lord is always ready to judge sin and to forgive sin by Calvary. He will forgive

81

any hour of the day or any day of the week. "The Lord is not slack concerning his promise, as some men count slackness; but is longsuffering to us-ward, not willing that any should perish, but that all should come to repentance" (II Peter 3:9).

5. *The original fire was from God.* After the first priests were consecrated for service and the first sacrifice was laid on the altar, a great miracle occurred: "And there came a fire out from before the LORD, and consumed upon the altar the burnt offering and the fat" (Leviticus 9:24). God initiated the original fire.

It is miraculous how that God can take a person who has been very wicked and has many things to feel condemned for and can completely remove all guilt. "There is therefore now no condemnation to them which are in Christ Jesus" (Romans 8:1). God is the initiator of repentance. "No man can come to me, except the Father which hath sent me draw him" (John 6:44).

God placed His approval upon the original sacrifice by sending fire. God approved the sacrifice of the man Christ Jesus by miraculous signs such as an earthquake, darkness, and the resurrection of saints. The greatest seal of approval was the resurrection of Christ. When we truly repent and exercise faith, the Lord will place His seal of approval by filling us with the Holy Ghost accompanied by the evidence of speaking with other tongues. "After that ye believed, ye were sealed with that holy Spirit of promise" (Ephesians 1:13).

WATER

After the brazen altar, the next piece of furniture was

the laver of water. *Laver* simply means "a place for washing." The laver was made from brass looking glasses or mirrors made of polished, solid brass. The Bible gives no description of the original size and shape of the laver. Its location was between the brazen altar and the entrance to the Holy Place, and it held water for the priest to wash with.

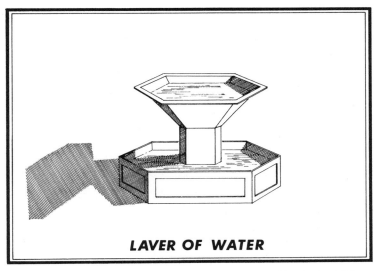

LAVER OF WATER

Here is the witness of water. How beautifully the Tabernacle plan provides a typology of repentance, water baptism and the baptism of the Holy Ghost at conversion. Clearly, the laver of water is a type of water baptism as the following points demonstrate.

1. *The laver's location and importance.* "And thou shalt put it between the tabernacle of the congregation and the altar. . . .they shall wash with water, that they die not" (Exodus 30:18, 20). The laver was located in such a way

that the one approaching would run right into it while walking forward to the Holy Place. The only way to avoid it was to walk around it.

God warned Aaron and his sons that if they entered into the Holy Place without washing they would die. This was a very dramatic measure God used to emphasize the importance of obedience and of a spiritual washing with water.

The New Testament is replete with exhortations to baptize as well as examples of baptism. After Cornelius and his household received the Holy Ghost, Peter "commanded them to be baptized in the name of the Lord" (Acts 10:48). He did not give them an option. To command means to order or enjoin with authority. Baptism is not to be viewed passively as if it were just an unnecessary formality.

2. *The laver was for washing.* After the priest butchered a sacrifice at the altar, his hands and feet would be covered with blood. The laver was provided for washing. God loves purity and cleanliness, not just of the outward man, but of the heart.

Baptism in water is for the washing away of sins: "Be baptized every one of you in the name of Jesus Christ for the remission of sins" (Acts 2:38). In other words, at baptism God removes, cancels or eradicates sin. Repentance and baptism together bring the complete work of forgiveness of sins.

The Apostle Paul, when giving his testimony at Jerusalem, reiterated the words of Ananias concerning his water baptism: "And now why tarriest thou? arise and be baptized, and wash away thy sins, calling on the name of the Lord" (Acts 22:16). Again, at baptism a repentant believer experiences the washing away of sins. Jesus commissioned the disciples to remit sin, and they did so through baptism. "Whose soever sins ye remit, they are remitted unto them" (John 20:23). Even the word *baptize* itself denotes a washing or an immersing with water.

3. *Made from looking glasses.* "And he made the laver of brass, and the foot of it of brass, of the lookingglasses of the women assembling" (Exodus 38:8). Polished brass mirrors were melted down and remade into a basin for water. The women gave up their mirrors, demonstrating humility and self-denial. The vanity of a proud person causes him look into a mirror frequently because of his great interest in himself.

Today it is a humbling thing for a person to be baptized in water. It is inconvenient. Baptism ruins a person's hairdo and makes quite a spectacle of him. Some churches have substituted sprinkling for immersion, thereby avoiding damage to their converts' haughty posture. If a person has truly repented, however, he has thrown away his pride and he considers it a great honor to be baptized (immersed). The old man is dead and is ready for burial. He has melted down his mirrors. The awkwardness and ungracefulness associated with water baptism only serve to heighten the experience.

4. *The priests washed their hands and feet.* "For Aaron and his sons shall wash their hands and their feet thereat" (Exodus 30:19). The hands and the feet are the two extremities of the anatomy that symbolize service and activity. As the priests washed themselves before entering the Holy Place, so a believer today must submit to the waters of baptism before he enters into the service of the Lord.

When Jesus washed His disciples' feet, Peter said,

"Thou shalt never wash my feet" (John 13:8). But when Jesus explained that Peter would then have no part with Him, Peter replied, "Lord, not my feet only, but also my hands and my head" (John 13:9). God loves that kind of eager spirit. We should seek to fulfill all of God's program instead of searching for minimum requirements. We should not be content to wade when there are waters deep enough to swim in (Ezekiel 47).

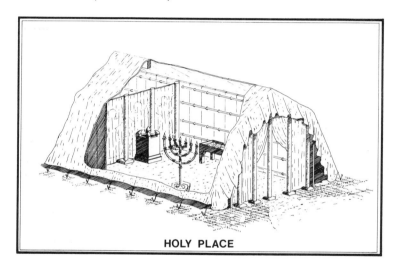

HOLY PLACE

SPIRIT

After a person passed the brazen altar and the laver of water in the Tabernacle courtyard, he came to the entrance of the Holy Place. Here again were linen curtains—scarlet, purple, blue and white—hanging from five pillars that were covered with gold.

Inside the room the beauty was breathtaking. The

walls were covered with pure gold. Overhead was a scarlet, purple, blue and white tapestry embroidered with cherubim. Straight ahead was a veil of linen dyed the same four colors with cherubim embroidered in the cloth.

On the south side of the room was the golden candlestick. To the north was the table of shewbread. Immediately before the veil was the altar of incense.

This place was dedicated to communion with God. The priest was shut in from the outside confusion as he ministered unto the Lord. Each piece of furniture was used for a particular function.

This room is a type of the Holy Ghost. It is a witness of the Spirit. The beauty of the room is a type of the beauty of the Holy Ghost. "He will beautify the meek with salvation" (Psalm 149:4). The gold walls represent the value of salvation, for salvation is a very precious gift. "The kingdom of heaven is like unto treasure hid in a field; the which when a man hath found, he hideth, and for joy thereof goeth and selleth all that he hath, and buyeth that field" (Matthew 13:44).

Each piece of furniture has its own special application as it relates to the baptism in the Holy Ghost and our ongoing relationship with God in the Spirit-filled life.

GOLDEN LAMPSTAND

The golden "candlestick," actually a standing oil lamp, was made from beaten gold. Its exact size is not given in Scripture, but it weighed one talent (estimated as 107 pounds). The entire lampstand was one piece, completely hollow inside. It had one main center shaft with six branching lamps, three on each side. It was decorated with engraved almond flowers. Its purpose was to give light to the priest as he ministered. This ornate lamp is a type of the Holy Ghost. The following brief points illustrate this analogy.

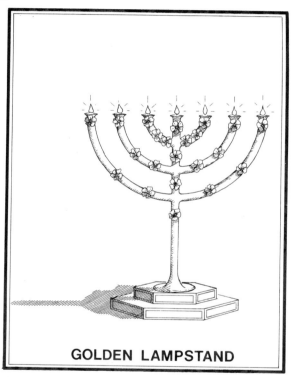

GOLDEN LAMPSTAND

1. *The lampstand gave light.* Jesus is the light of the world (John 9:5). When we receive the Holy Ghost we have Jesus Christ in us (Colossians 1:27). The Holy Ghost gives us spiritual illumination. First, the Spirit enables us to shine before the world: "Let your light so shine before men, that

they may see your good works, and glorify your Father which is in heaven" (Matthew 5:16). Second, the Spirit gives us sensitivity of conscience to distinguish right from wrong. In other words, the light shines inward, revealing the inner man. Third, the Holy Ghost illuminates the Word of God. We acquire a perception that we did not have before we received the Holy Ghost. "But the Comforter, which is the Holy Ghost, . . .he shall teach you all things" (John 14:26).

2. *The lampstand represents the church.* "The seven candlesticks which thou sawest are the seven churches" (Revelation 1:20). We must have the Holy Ghost to be in the church. "Now if any man have not the Spirit of Christ, he is none of his" (Romans 8:9). Spiritfilled believers can be compared to the six branches. Six is often considered to be man's number as it is one short of seven, God's number of completion and perfection. Jesus can be compared to the center shaft, the seventh light that makes the others complete. Jesus is the vine and we are the branches (John 15:5). We "are complete in him, which is the head of all principality and power" (Colossians 2:10).

3. *The oil is a type of the Holy Ghost.* Oil is a type of the Holy Ghost throughout the Word of God. (See Matthew 25:1-13, Hebrews 1:9, Leviticus 8:10-12, I Samuel 10:1.) The lamp was hollow. When oil was poured into one branch, it would diffuse into all seven branches equally. The Holy Ghost that was poured out at Pentecost is the same today as it was then (Hebrews 13:8).

The oil provided fuel for the light. The Holy Ghost is the source of power and light in our life. "But ye shall receive power, after that the Holy Ghost is come upon you" (Acts 1:8). If we will be the wick, staying in the lampstand (the church) and soaking up the oil of the Holy Ghost, we will produce light to the world.

The olive oil was to be pure. We are not to seek after spiritual substitutes and counterfeits, such as mysticism, but after the Holy Spirit.

4. *The lamp was continually filled.* "Aaron and his sons shall order it from evening to morning before the LORD" (Exodus 27:21). The wicks were to be trimmed and new oil poured into the lampstand every morning and evening. One experience with the Lord is not enough. We are admonished, "Be not drunk with wine, wherein is excess; but be filled with the Spirit" (Ephesians 5:18). We need that recurrent and continual filling of the oil of the Spirit.

TABLE OF SHEWBREAD

On the north side of the Holy Place stood a little table made of acacia wood covered with gold. It was eighteen inches wide by thirty-six inches long. For carrying, it had rings of gold and poles overlaid with gold. The dishes, spoons, pitchers, and flagons were also made of gold. Each Sabbath, twelve loaves of bread were placed on the table for the priest to eat as he ministered in the Holy Place. A molding around the top edge of the table served to prevent the loaves from being knocked off. The little table was only twenty-seven inches high.

The table of shewbread—literally, "the bread of the Presence"—is a type of reading, studying and memorizing the Word of God after receiving the Holy Ghost. After a person receives the baptism of the Holy Ghost, the Word comes alive with meaning and inspiration and nourishes his spiritual life. Several truths about the Spirit-filled life can be gleaned from this type.

TABLE OF SHEWBREAD

1. *The priest ate bread while ministering in the Holy Place.* The bread was eaten in the Holy Place. The priest was separated from the camp of Israel in this lovely room of solitude. Likewise, when we read the Bible we must be in a spiritual frame of mind. It is a spiritual book and the carnal mind cannot understand it. We must be sensitive in order for the Holy Ghost to assist our understanding. "The natural man receiveth not the things of the Spirit of God: for they are foolishness unto him: neither can he know them, because they are spiritually discerned" (I Corinthians 2:14).

The bread gave strength and nourishment to the priest. Just to be in the Holy Place (to have the Holy Ghost) is not enough. By studying the Word of God our spiritual man receives strength.

2. *The bread was fresh.* The loaves were made fresh every Sabbath day. The bread was not allowed to become old and moldy. Times of refreshing must come to the Spirit-filled child of God to renew his hunger for the Bread of Life. We cannot live on an occasional meal from the Word of God. "Study to shew thyself approved unto God, a workman that needeth not to be ashamed" (II Timothy 2:15). We must partake daily.

3. *The quantity of bread.* Each loaf was made from "two tenth deals" of fine flour (Leviticus 24:5). Twelve loaves were placed on the table in two rows. One-tenth was the amount in an omer. While the Israelites were in the wilderness, they were allowed one omer of manna each day. This lets us know that there was plenty of bread for the priest.

There is no excuse for us to go hungry for the Word of God. The Lord has preserved the Bible through the years though many have attacked it. The Bible is freely available to all of us today. The Bible contains many principles of life as well as many inspirational loaves to satisfy our spiritual hunger.

4. *The table was only twenty-seven inches high.* This low table required the priest to stoop to reach the bread. The Word of God is available to those who humble themselves. "I thank thee, O Father, Lord of heaven and earth, that thou hast hid these things from the wise and prudent, and hast revealed them unto babes" (Luke 10:21).

5. *The bread was made from fine flour.* The recipe given for the bread in Leviticus 24 says it was to be made from "fine flour." No fancy ingredients were to be added. God's Word is forever settled in heaven (Psalm 119:89). We can add nothing to it.

6. *The bread was eaten.* The process of eating involves chewing, swallowing and digesting food. Reading the Word of God also involves a process. The Bible does us no good on the shelf. Speed reading may have its place, but not when reading the Bible. As a cow chews her cud at the end of the day, so we must meditate on the Word of God in order for the spiritual man to digest it.

ALTAR OF INCENSE

This small altar sat against the veil in the Holy Place. It was made of acacia wood and covered with gold. The thirty-six-inch-high altar was eighteen inches square with a horn at each top corner. Incense was burned every morning and evening upon the altar of incense.

The activity around this altar is a type of prayer and worship. The psalmist said, "Let my prayer be set forth

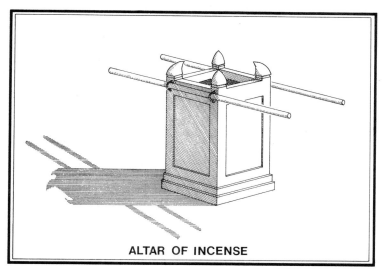

ALTAR OF INCENSE

before thee as incense; and the lifting up of my hands as the evening sacrifice" (Psalm 141:2). The Book of Revelation compares the prayers of the saints to the burning incense at the altar (Revelation 5:8). "And the smoke of the incense, which came with the prayers of the saints, ascended up before God" (Revelation 8:4).

The baptism of the Holy Ghost is necessary for effectiveness in prayer and worship. We have power in prayer when we allow the Spirit to assist us (Romans 8:26-27). "The effectual fervent prayer of a righteous man availeth much" (James 5:16).

The following points show how the altar of incense is a type of our worship and prayer in the Holy Ghost.

1. *The altar of incense was near the veil.* Immediately behind the altar was the veil, and behind the veil was the Holiest of Holies, a type of heaven. We are very close to God when we pray. Prayer is our first step to God. There is no other approach to the throne of God but through prayer. Even though we are on earth, when we pray we are at the veil of heaven.

John said, "I was in the Spirit on the Lord's day" (Revelation 1:10). While in prayer he saw many heavenly things. When Stephen looked upward, full of the Holy Ghost, he saw the glory of God and Jesus standing on the right hand of God (Acts 7:55). Praying and worshiping in the Spirit is the closest thing on earth to experiencing heaven.

2. *The burning incense produced a sweet odor.* The apothecaries ground and mixed together four sweet spices for the incense: stacte, onycha, galbanum and frankincense. Fire from the brazen altar was placed upon the altar of incense and the incense was sprinkled over the hot coals.

This produced a sweet perfume which filled the Holy Place and drifted out into the courtyard. This composition of spices was not to be duplicated for any other, common use (Exodus 30:34-38).

The Lord loves to have His children pray and worship. Just as earthly parents love the fellowship of their children, God loves our daily sacrifice of prayer and worship. It is a sweet savor unto Him.

3. *The priest burned incense by the light of the lampstand.* "And Aaron shall burn thereon sweet incense every morning: when he dresseth the lamps, he shall burn incense upon it. And when Aaron lighteth the lamps at even, he shall burn incense upon it" (Exodus 30:7-8). The light of the lampstand gave light to the priest at the altar of incense. The light of the Holy Ghost gives us spiritual insight and aid when we pray. "Likewise the Spirit also helpeth our infirmities: for we know not what we should pray for as we ought: but the Spirit itself maketh intercession for us with groanings which cannot be uttered" (Romans 8:26). Having the Holy Ghost gives us the assistance of God's Spirit in prayer. An effective prayer life is impossible without the Holy Ghost.

4. *The altar of incense had horns.* A horn made of pure gold was situated at each corner of the altar. Horns in the Bible are symbolic of power. (See Psalm 75:4, 10; 89:17; 92:10.) The Holy Ghost is a source of power to the Christian. "But ye shall receive power, after that the Holy Ghost is come upon you" (Acts 1:8). Jesus was speaking of power to witness, but not only to witness verbally. We are given power to be a living witness that Jesus delivers from sin. We have power over temptation and power in prayer and worship.

5. *No strange fire or strange incense was to be used.* "Ye shall offer no strange incense thereon" (Exodus 30:9). Everything was to be done exactly in accordance with God's plan. Nadab and Abihu offered strange fire on the altar and were burned up by fire from God (Leviticus 10). Since fire from the brazen altar was supposed to be used, Nadab and Abihu evidently brought fire from another source.

Our prayer and worship should be backed by repentance and consecration. Jesus told the woman at the well of Samaria that everyone must worship God in spirit and in truth (John 4:24). We should become involved wholeheartedly in prayer and worship, and this should always come from a life that is true to God.

FOOTNOTES

[1]C. Sumner Wemp, *Teaching from the Tabernacle* (Chicago: Moody Press, 1976), p. 13.

[2]Robert Coleman, *Written in Blood* (Old Tappan, N.J.: Fleming H. Revell, 1972), pp. 27-28.

6.

The Natural Birth As God's Witness

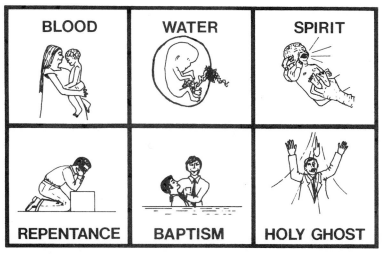

BLOOD	WATER	SPIRIT
REPENTANCE	BAPTISM	HOLY GHOST

"Jesus answered and said unto him, Verily, verily, I say unto thee, Except a man be born again, he cannot see the kingdom of God. Nicodemus saith unto him, How can a man be born when he is old? can he enter the second time into his mother's womb, and be born? Jesus answered, Verily, verily, I say unto thee, Except a man be born of water and of the Spirit, he cannot enter into the kingdom of God" (John 3:3-5).

*N*icodemus was a Jewish religious leader. He later defended Jesus when Pharisees rebuked their guards for not arresting Him (John 7:50-53). Nicodemus, along with Joseph of Arimathea, asked Pilate for the body of Jesus and buried it in a new tomb (John 19:38-42).

Such displays of loyalty offer convincing evidence that Nicodemus was sincere in his pursuit of Jesus by night. Perhaps he wanted a private meeting with this new teacher without interruption from the crowd. Alone with Jesus, he could ask the most difficult questions and feel comfortable that they would be answered thoroughly in the quiet peacefulness of the night. Or perhaps it was a covert approach to avoid problems with his peers. Maybe he wanted to be sure about his feelings concerning the miracle worker before publically confessing faith in Him.

Whatever his motive, Jesus did not disappoint him. Nicodemus privately received a beautiful explanation of the gospel. Jesus introduced to him a new analogy from New Testament salvation: "Ye must be born again" (John 3:7). Jesus compared conversion from sin to the kingdom of God to being "born again."

By using this comparison, Jesus emphasized the necessity of change. Since the old life is sinful and fallen from its relation with God, it must die. To be saved, a person must undergo a spiritual transformation; he must die to the old life and be resurrected to a new life. "Therefore if any man be in Christ, he is a new creature: old things are passed away; behold, all things are become new" (II Corinthians 5:17). The salvation experience is so revolutionary and glorious in its life-changing effect that without exaggeration, it can be called a new birth.

Jesus did not offer the new birth as an option. To the contrary, He stated the necessity of the new birth in bold terms: "Except a man be born again, he cannot see the kingdom of God" (John 3:3). "Ye must be born again" (John 3:7). Aliens cannot receive naturalized citizenship into God's kingdom, they have to become natural born citizens. "That which is born of the flesh is flesh; and that which is born of the Spirit is spirit" (John 3:6).

God refuses to make garments from patchwork. He will not sew His new seamless cloth into the threadbare, rotten rags of the sinful nature. Nor will He pour the pure vintage wine of the Holy Ghost into the old, crusty wine skins of carnality (Mark 2:21-22). The new cannot be mixed with the old, lest the new be spoiled by the decay of the old.

WATER AND SPIRIT

Nicodemus asked Jesus the meaning of this rebirth, pointing out the impossibility of naturally being reborn from his mother's womb. In response, Jesus explained the necessity of birth by water and Spirit.

It is important to remember that at the time John the Baptist was actively preaching the need to repent, be baptized in water and look for the One who would baptize with the Holy Spirit. As were all the Jewish religious leaders, Nicodemus was familiar with John's ministry. Clearly, then,

Jesus was describing baptism by His reference to water. He also thereby included repentance, for John preached "the baptism of repentance" and required all baptismal candidates to confess their sins and repent before he would baptize them (Mark 1:4-5; Luke 3:7-8).

Some try to minimize the importance of baptism by saying that water refers merely to the natural birth, since an unborn child is suspended in amniotic fluid. It seems ridiculous, however, to think Jesus was telling Nicodemus that a person must be born physically to enter the kingdom of God. There is absolutely no indication that the Pharisees believed in the pre-existence of souls or believed that the unborn could have a relationship with God prior to this life. Considering the fame of John the Baptist at this time and the New Testament church's practice of baptism it is clear that water meant repentance and water baptism.

Not only was Jesus confirming the ministry and message of John the Baptist but he was also revealing to Nicodemus the coming of the baptism of the Holy Ghost. The Spirit birth also was to be part of conversion. This message was in perfect harmony with John's preaching. "I indeed baptize you with water; but one mightier than I cometh, the latchet of whose shoes I am not worthy to unloose: he shall baptize you with the Holy Ghost and with fire" (Luke 3:16).

In considering the analogy set forth by Jesus, we discover that the conversion experience is beautifully illustrated by the natural birth of a child. Here again we find the witness of blood, water and Spirit.

BLOOD

In many instances, the words *blood* and *death* are

used interchangeably. Blood reminds us of suffering and discomfort.

The process of childbirth is one of the most painful, excruciating experiences a mother will have in life. "Unto the woman he said, I will greatly multiply thy sorrow and thy conception; in sorrow thou shalt bring forth children" (Genesis 3:16).

Usually, one of the first effects of pregnancy is "morning sickness." The little new life begins to draw life from the mother and to reveal many evidences of its presence. For approximately nine months there is a continual weight gain until some mothers wonder if they will ever look normal again. Expectant mothers restrict their activities and take precautions that normally would not be necessary. They require more rest as well as closer consideration of correct diet. Susceptibility to little nagging inconveniences such as dizzy spells, swelling, varicose veins and cramps plagues many expectant mothers. The process is a great sacrifice on the part of the mother.

The process of labor and the birth of the child is the time of greatest pain. Thanks to modern medicine, the doctor usually administers a pain-relieving drug when the pain becomes severe, something that was not available many years ago.

The mother uses her body's strength and resources, sacrificing her health for a new life. It is impossible to alter the basic process of childbirth. It has been designed by God. It simply must be the way it is.

Just as the natural birth requires a giving of one's self, so does the new birth. Before a person can be born again, a death must come first. The old man must die to self-interest and ambition. He must turn away from sin and repent in order to foster new life in himself. "Let the wicked forsake his way, and the unrighteous man his thoughts: and let him return unto the LORD, and he will have mercy upon him; and to our God, for he will abundantly pardon" (Isaiah 55:7).

To the natural eye, the birth of a child is not an occasion of beauty, grace or charm. "Reduced to its simplest constituents, the process of labor resolves itself into the expulsion from the uterus of the products of conception, that is, the baby, afterbirth, membranes and fluid." [1] Most fathers are terrified at the possibility of being alone with their wife at the time of delivery. Due to a lack of understanding and skill, the father is usually ill-equipped to handle such a predicament.

The experience of repentance is a time of crucifixion of the old nature. Sorrow for past sins brings tears. "For godly sorrow worketh repentance to salvation" (II Corinthians 7:10). Tearing away from the past life is a very traumatic experience. The old man is wounded and fights for life. This war of the flesh may go on for days or even weeks before the death is finally complete. On the other hand, some make a total commitment immediately and conquer the old man in repentance quickly. Those who prolong this death to self become very miserable. Their indecisiveness only leads to a raging war between flesh and Spirit. Only by completing the spiritual death can a person live again. "Repent ye therefore, and be converted, that your sins may be blotted out, when the times of refreshing shall come from the presence of the Lord" (Acts 3:19).

WATER
The first nine months of every human life is spent in

the shadowy, warm, watery world of the mother's womb.

Only two weeks after the ovum has been fertilized, water is surrounding the tiny new life:

> *The balloon-like sac of water which surrounds and protects you [is] still smaller than the seed of an apple. . . .Some cells have gathered and formed a bubble-like sac which is filled with fluid. This sac is called the amnion, which is a Greek term meaning "little lamb," chosen because lambs are often born enclosed in these prenatal membranes and fluid. This "bag of waters" will cushion, protect, insulate, and provide free movement to the developing individual.* [2]

After the third month of development, the fetus "breathes" the amniotic fluid regularly to exercise and develop the respiratory system. The child also drinks the fluid and digests it.

Occasionally labor is initiated by rupture of the amniotic sac. In such an event, it is time to prepare for the birth of the child.

This aspect of natural birth parallels our water baptism. In accordance with New Testament teaching and examples, we are immersed into a watery grave at baptism. As the meaning of the word *baptism* indicates, we are immersed into the water—completely surrounded and engulfed. The witness of water is a necessary part of the new birth experience.

SPIRIT

One of the most awesome and wonderful natural occurences is the birth of a human being. It brings the parents a most exultant feeling of happiness as they experience the joy of bringing a new baby into the world. The birth process occurs as follows:

> *The act of birth is thought to be triggered by a complexity of processes. A unilateral "decision" is made by the mature fetus and communicated electro-chemically from his brain to the aging placenta, which is also changing hormonally, and which, in turn, notifies the uterus. The contractions and the labor begin.*
>
> *The uterine muscles contract and eventually the mother is allowed to "bear down." Pressures of up to one hundred pounds push and propel the infant through the birth canal and out into his new environment. The jelly in the umbilical cord begins to swell immediately upon contact with air, restricting flow to the placenta and forcing the infant's blood to its own lungs for oxygen. As the baby gasps and air sweeps into the lungs and fills the thousands of tiny air sacs, a first cry is vocalized.*[3]

A child can be perfectly normal in every way, but unless it begins to breathe, it will not live. One of the major problems with premature infants is poorly developed lungs. If the child cannot breathe, it will die.

This transition to new life parallels the new birth in the Spirit. The child before birth receives oxygen from the mother through the umbilical cord. But at the moment of birth it must break that dependence upon its mother. The umbilical cord begins to close off its supply to the child, forcing it to breathe air into its lungs.

After a person has repented of his sins and been baptized in water in the name of the Lord Jesus Christ, he must be filled with the Spirit. This breathing in of the Holy Spirit completes the new birth experience. He has not been born again until he receives the Holy Spirit.

This is the final break with the old nature. No longer does he need an umbilical cord. Once a baby begins to breathe, the doctor will cut the cord and the infant will begin life independent of its mother. The child is now dependent upon the breath of air to sustain its life. After we are born again, we then become dependent upon the Spirit and not the flesh. "But ye shall receive power, after that the Holy Ghost is come upon you" (Acts 1:8).

The baptism of the Holy Ghost is the very breath of the Lord. "He [Jesus] breathed on them, and saith unto them, Receive ye the Holy Ghost" (John 20:22). The Lord Jesus was signifying that the Holy Ghost would be His very breath of spiritual life upon and within them.

Breathing is an involuntary function of the human body. We do not have to consciously tell our lungs to breathe. If a person has fully repented, has been baptized and opens his heart in faith, the filling of the Holy Ghost will occur naturally. "Repent, and be baptized every one of you in the name of Jesus Christ for the remission of sins, and ye shall receive the gift of the Holy Ghost" (Acts 2:38).

John the Baptist, speaking of the Spirit birth, said, "He shall baptize you with the Holy Ghost, and with fire" (Matthew 3:11). Just as a child is surrounded or baptized by water before birth, after birth it is surrounded or baptized by air. That is why being filled with the Holy Ghost is called a baptism. We are baptized from above. "And, behold, I send the promise of my Father upon you: but tarry ye in the city of Jerusalem, until ye be endued with power from on high" (Luke 24:49).

A doctor is not satisfied until he hears the newborn cry. Vocal cords are developed when the fetus is only three months old. If there is no cry, the doctor will give the infant a spat on the posterior which will always activate a squawk of frustration in a healthy baby. A newborn babe in Christ will also show signs of life. There will be a cry heard giving evidence of the Holy Ghost's presence. He will begin to speak with other tongues as the Spirit gives the utterance. "And these signs shall follow them that believe; In my name shall they cast out devils; they shall speak with new tongues" (Mark 16:17). The prophet Isaiah said, "For with stammering lips and another tongue will he speak to this people" (Isaiah 28:11).

The New Testament believers in the following places spoke in tongues when they received the Holy Ghost:

1. *Jerusalem, on the Day of Pentecost* (Acts 2:4). "And they were all filled with the Holy Ghost, and began to speak with other tongues, as the Spirit gave them utterance." As many as eighteen different languages were spoken by these 120 newly baptized believers. They spoke in intelligible languages and were understood by the crowd.

2. *Samaria* (Acts 8:18). "And when Simon saw that through laying on of the apostles' hands the Holy Ghost was given, he offered them money." Simon had seen miracles, unclean spirits cast out, palsied people healed, lame people healed and great joy in the city. He also had seen water baptisms. Even Simon had been baptized. But when he saw people receive the Holy Ghost by the laying on of

the apostles' hands, he offered to purchase that power. Something remarkable happened to those people as they received the Holy Ghost. What was it that aroused such desire in Simon? A comparison with the other accounts shows that they must have been speaking in tongues.

3. *Caesarea* (Acts 10:45-46). "On the Gentiles also was poured out the gift of the Holy Ghost. For they heard them speak with tongues, and magnify God." Speaking in tongues was the confirming evidence that the Gentiles had received the Holy Ghost just as at Pentecost.

4. *Ephesus* (Acts 19:6). "And when Paul had laid his hands upon them, the Holy Ghost came on them; and they spake with tongues, and prophesied." These apostles of John the Baptist spoke with tongues when they received the Holy Ghost.

"In the mouth of two or three witnesses shall every word be established" (II Corinthians 13:1).

FOOTNOTES

[1]Nicholson Eastman, M.D., and Keith Russell, M.D., *Expectant Motherhood* (Boston: Little, Brown and Co., 1970), p. 144.

[2]Gary Bergel and C. Everett Koop, M.D., *When You were Formed in Secret* (Elyria, Ohio: Intercessors for American, 1980), p. 1-15.

[3]Ibid., p. 1-15.

7.

The Miracle Of The Seed As God's Witness

DEATH	BURIAL	RESURRECTION
REPENTANCE	BAPTISM	HOLY GHOST

"Verily, verily, I say unto you, Except a corn of wheat fall into the ground and die, it abideth alone: but if it die, it bringeth forth much fruit" (John 12:24).

In my childhood, I lived on a farm. Every year, my father mounted the old tractor and attempted to conquer our small acreage in Keithville, Louisiana. Since field peas were a staple on our table, there was always a large patch of these nutritious green pods to be cared for.

My father was not satisfied with the particular strain he was raising, so a number of varieties were tried: "brown crowders," "purple hulls," "cream peas," and "red rippers." None of these seemed to suit my father. Finally, a friend came along and offered to help with yet another variety.

They were planted in the spring and grew wonderfully. They blossomed on time, the vines were healthy, and the pods were long and full. The part I liked most was the ease with which they could be shelled. After my mother served the first dish of these little smooth seeds, the decision was unanimous. We had found a palatable little pea that would grace our table for many years to come.

Surely, we thought, such an amazing little pea would have an appropriate name such as "marvelous gems," "heavenly pride" or "angel pods." Yet my father was told that they were just called "John Browns." No one knew where they came from or how they were named. The local seed store had never heard of them. Because of the lost pedigree, it was necessary to save some of the seeds for future planting.

After the canning season had ended, I was allowed

111

to pursue other things, which was a great relief from the world of picking and shelling peas. In the busy activity of my childhood games, however, I did notice the forethought my father had concerning the peas.

The heat and dryness of the summer began to set in. The verdant vines began to wither and die. Soon the leaves turned brown and many fell to the ground. The pea patch became an ugly scene of tangled dead vines with ugly brown pods hanging from the stems.

My father, with his tow sack, began the job of collecting the remaining pods. After filling several sacks, he returned to the barn and there began to do some very interesting things. He took a bat and, with the burlap sack securely tied, began to beat the dry peas. As the peas were beaten, the brittle hulls began to break up, emptying their contents. After determining the job was done by feeling the loose peas in the bottom of the sack, the next phase of preservation began. He placed a large fan where it would blow a current of air past the peas as they fell from the sack to a container on the ground. The dry hulls were blown away, while the little seeds were kept for the next season.

The seeds were wrinkled and dry. All signs of life were gone. Their hardness and lack of moisture made them easy to store. They were placed in a large jar, which was sprinkled with poison and sealed tightly to protect the seeds from weevils and moisture.

In the spring, after the field had been plowed and rows made up, Dad went to the shelf for the precious seed. After the ground was fertilized, the seeds were sprinkled on the warm moist earth. When the seeds were sown, the tractor, with its cultivator plow, completely covered them with dirt.

Within a week most of the little seeds had begun to show signs of life. Tiny cracks formed in the soil as tender little shoots forced their way to the surface. The pale green shoots turned to dark green leaves and, with time, the rows were wrapped up with lush vines. Before long I was back in the field with my straw bushel basket, picking peas.

The germination of a seed is one of the most astounding miracles of life. It so beautifully illustrates the steps of our conversion from death to life. We must die to the flesh and be buried in a watery grave in order to rise to newness of life.

DEATH
"For if we be dead with him, we shall also live with him" (II Timothy 2:11).

Spring planting and the harvest season are two very exciting times, but the death of seeds is not a celebrated occasion. Many times it goes completely unnoticed. The plant is in most cases at its ugliest stage.

The repentance experience is much the same. It is a death to selfish desires. It involves a surrendering of the will. It does not remove our will, but it molds the will to align with God's will.

The death of a seed is necessary before it will germinate. If a pea seed is buried in the earth while it is still green, it will simply rot and decay. Likewise, repentance must precede baptism for baptism to be effective at that time. A person who is baptized without repentance is just getting wet. Some people think that baptism alone brings certain favor with God. But baptism without repentance is to no avail.

Nearly all seeds thrive best if they are planted less than a year after they have ripened. This time period allows nature's process to do its work. Our repentance experience must be complete and total. Many have fallen back into sin because they made their commitment too hastily and without enough consideration and commitment.

Some seeds keep longer than others. Corn will germinate readily after two years, but if not planted in three to four years, it will die. Wheat has been known to germinate after thirty years. Most seeds will not keep over a long period of time however.

After we have repented, we should proceed in our obedience to the gospel. Waiting too long to be baptized and to receive the Holy Ghost will cause a person to continue in a rut of doubt. His faith will become stymied and it will become more and more difficult for him to receive a new life experience.

When a pea seed dies, the little fiber that gives it life is broken, leaving a little brown spot. Most seeds have a mark on them somewhere indicating that broken life source. When a person decides to live for God, his life cord with the world must be broken. The umbilical cord must be cut. Separation from the world will hurt and perhaps will leave a tiny scar of broken friendships and lost worldly gains. But the sacrifice is well worth the great rewards of the new life.

BURIAL

"For if we have been planted together in the likeness of his death, we shall be also in the likeness of his resurrection" (Romans 6:5)

The Scriptures plainly state that baptism in water is a burial with Christ. "Buried with him in baptism" (Colossians 2:12). "Therefore we are buried with him by baptism into death" (Romans 6:4).

Every farmer knows the importance of completely covering the seed at planting time. Not covering the seed would expose it for the birds to come immediately and devour it. The seed also needs the moisture from the earth that it would not get on the surface. The moisture in the ground softens the skin of the seed and swells the tissue of the embryo. The moisture or water also helps to dissolve certain food materials in the seed so they can be used for growth.

One of the main reasons then, for a seed to be planted beneath the soil is to put it in contact with water. In fact, the germination process can be enhanced by soaking the seed in water before planting. Once again, we have the witness of water.

Since baptism is a type of burial, immersion is the Bible's way to be baptized. The following examples of Bible baptisms show that immersion, not sprinkling, was the practice of the Early Church.

1. *John at Aenon* (John 3:23). "John also was baptizing in Aenon near to Salim, because there was much water there." Aenon means "natural fountains." It was a place at the head of the valley of Shechem, fed by copious springs. John located there because "there was much water there." Obviously he did not need "much water" if he only planned to sprinkle or pour a small amount of water on each convert.

2. *Baptism of Jesus* (Matthew 3:16). "And Jesus, when he was baptized, went up straightway out of the wat-

er." First of all, this baptism was in the Jordan River. It seems foolish to think that John would have chosen the river for his baptisms if he only needed to sprinkle a little water upon each convert. Second, this verse indicates the movement of the body of Jesus as He was baptized. When a person is sprinkled, there is no movement necessary on the part of the one being baptized.

3. *Ethiopian eunuch and Philip* (Acts 8:38-39). "They went down both into the water. . .and he baptized him. And when they were come up out of the water, the Spirit of the Lord caught away Philip." This event happened on the road from Jerusalem to Gaza, "which is desert" (Acts 8:26). Evidently they came upon an oasis with a pool of water large enough for two men to go down into. Here again, the circumstances indicate baptism by immersion.

4. *Baptism unto Moses* (I Corinthians 10:1-2). "Our fathers were under the cloud, and all passed through the sea; and were all baptized unto Moses in the cloud and in the sea." Israel's passing through the sea is compared to the act of baptism. The Israelites walked on the bottom of the sea bed with water rising above them on either side. "And the children of Israel went into the midst of the sea upon the dry ground: and the waters were a wall unto them on their right hand, and on their left" (Exodus 14:22). This type represents more than just sprinkling.

Even the word *baptize* in the New Testament is translated from the Greek word *baptizo,* which means to immerse, dip, plunge or submerge. If baptism practiced by the New Testament church had been sprinkling, the Greek word *rantizo* would have been used.

RESURRECTION

The germination of a seed is one of the most astounding events in nature. Something that seems completely dead begins to live again. Man has accomplished many remarkable things, but that little invisible spark of life is something only God can create.

After the seed is planted, the farmer waits with great anticipation for the seed to sprout. He feels great relief when he sees the small cracks in the soil as the little sprout pushes back against the earth.

The warm moisture in the soil causes things to begin to happen in the little seed. It swells and then cracks open. A little shoot moves downward, which later develops into a root system. Another little shoot moves upward. After it surfaces into the sunlight, it begins to unfold into leaves. At this stage the new plant has just begun its new, visible life in the reproductive cycle.

Nothing is more disappointing to the farmer than to prepare the ground and plant the seed and then not to have it come up. If the seed does not sprout, there will be no harvest.

Our salvation is not complete without the resurrection experience. When we are filled with the Holy Ghost, we receive life to begin growing in the Lord. Our old man cannot produce the fruit of the Spirit. It only produces the works of the flesh. "But the fruit of the Spirit is love, joy, peace, longsuffering, gentleness, goodness, faith, meekness, temperance: against such there is no law" (Galatians 5:22-23).

There are people who naturally have good virtues. They may be gentle just by the nature of their personality. Unless the Holy Ghost is the motivating source, however, all their virtues are merely self-righteousness and cannot save them. "All our righteousnesses are as filthy rags" (Isaiah 64:6). "By the works of the law shall no flesh be justified" (Galatians 2:16). Only the Lord's righteousness can save us, and He wants all the fruit we produce to glorify Him. "Let your light so shine before men, that they may see your good works, and glorify your Father which is in heaven" (Matthew 5:16).

Just as the little green sprout is the beginning of the plant, our rebirth experience is just the beginning of a very exciting life of growth and maturity. Not only are we able to produce spiritual fruit, but we also can receive and exercise various spiritual gifts (Romans 12:6-8; I Corinthians 12). Our Christian life becomes more than a mere struggle to survive ("staying saved"); it becomes a life of ministering to the body of Christ.

8.

The Witness At Calvary

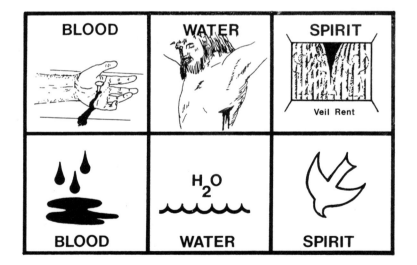

*N*o event in history inspires such pathos as the six hours Jesus Christ hung suspended on the cross. Never has there been such a short period of time so laden with meaning and accomplishment. At the hill called Golgotha, the place of the skull, the Messiah was lifted up and God's redemptive plan reached its apex. Although Christ's words were few, the crescendo of Calvary magnified every utterance with meaning. These significant moments present to every person the witness of blood, water, and Spirit.

During this sacred occasion, many prophecies were fulfilled by Jesus as well as by those who participated in His crucifixion. Many profound events occurred that day. Miracles accompanied the Lord's hours on the cross. The earth quaked, rocks were rent and there was darkness from noon until three p.m. The veil in the temple was torn from top to bottom. Many deceased saints were resurrected and reappeared in the streets. So profound were the events of that day that the Roman centurion who helped crucify Jesus said, "Truly this was the Son of God" (Matthew 27:54).

With the importance of Calvary in mind, it is significant that there we find the witness of blood, water and Spirit.

BLOOD
"And, having made peace through the blood of his cross, by him to reconcile all things unto himself" (Colossians 1:20).

121

There is only one mention of blood in the Bible's description of Christ's six hours on the cross (John 19:34), but clearly He lost great amounts of blood because of the scourging and the nails through His hands and feet. The earth at the base of the cross must have been stained with the Lord's precious blood. No doubt His face was streaked with coagulated blood from the piercing of the thorns. There is nothing so obvious at Calvary as the witness of blood.

Throughout the Old Testament, blood was sacred. The heart and the blood were symbolic of the divine essence of life. The Israelites were not to drink blood or eat anything strangled. When they killed an animal, they were to pour out its blood on the ground and cover that blood with earth (Leviticus 17:13). This was not only true in religious applications but in everyday activity, as a symbol of death and burial.

The blood shed from Emmanuel's veins was not just the life fluid of an ordinary man. "God gave His breath to man in creation, and His blood for man on Calvary. He gave His blood because He had given His breath. Each was His very life."[1]

In the words of songwriter Lanny Wolfe:

So many years
So many lambs were offered up
But all the blood that was spilled
Could never fill that bitter cup
Till one spotless Lamb in the form of man
Gave His life on Calvary
His was the only blood
That could ever set me free

For His blood was not just blood
Of another spotless lamb
But His blood was precious blood
For it washed the sins of man
And His blood heals my body
It sets my spirit free
And I'm so glad His precious blood
Still flows from Calvary[2]

This reminds us once again of our need to repent. To identify with the Lord's suffering requires a spiritual death to self. "The sacrifices of God are a broken spirit: a broken and a contrite heart, O God, thou wilt not despise" (Psalm 51:17).

BLOOD AND WATER
"But when they came to Jesus and saw that
he was dead already, they brake not his legs: but
one of the soldiers with a spear pierced his side,
and forthwith came there out blood and water"
(John 19:33-34).

Jesus died sooner than the two thieves crucified with Him, perhaps as a result of the beating and mockery His humanity had endured. Also, He did not fight to live but gave His life willingly. His quick death allowed prophecy to be fulfilled: "A bone of him shall not be broken. And again another scripture saith, They shall look on him whom they pierced" (John 19:36-37).

John is the only Gospel writer who recorded this outstanding occurrence. Of the four writers, he was the only eyewitness to the crucifixion and, under the inspiration of the Spirit, he attached great importance to this unusual expulsion of blood and water from the same wound. In his first epistle, the same apostle again referred to this event as a very considerable thing. "This is he that came by water and blood, even Jesus Christ, not by water only, but by water and blood. . . .And there are three that bear witness in earth, the Spirit, and the water, and the blood: and these three agree in one" (I John 5:6, 8)

The crucifixion fell during Passover week. At six p.m. on the day of the crucifixion the Sabbath began. The Jews requested of Pilate that the legs of those crucified be broken to hasten their death so the bodies could be removed before the Sabbath began. When it was discovered that Jesus was already dead, a soldier thrust a spear into the side of Jesus, perhaps to confirm the certainty of His death. Out of the wound came water and blood.

This seems to indicate that Jesus died from a broken heart. At least this is the conclusion of many medical authorities. Robert Coleman explained that apparently, during the suffering on the cross, Christ's heart swelled until it burst. Blood poured into the enlarged pericardium (the sac surrounding the heart), where it "separated into red clots and watery serum. When the distended sac was punctured by the soldier's spear, the water and blood discharged."[3]

A similar explanation is given by Dr. Stuart Bergsma, a physician and surgeon: "A small amount of pericardial fluid, up to 20 or 30 cc's, normally is present in good health. It is possible that with a wound piercing the pericardium and heart, enough pericardial fluid might escape to be described as water."[4] Concerning post-mortem findings, he says that several cases of ruptured hearts show "the

124

pericardial cavity was occupied by approximately 500 cc's of fluid and freshly clotted blood."[5]

The blood and water at Calvary are just another reminder of our death in repentance and the application of water in baptism. It is very profound that while Christ yet hung on the cross, He ordained another witness to the shared experience of blood and water. This displays once again what He has *done* for us as well as what He is doing *in* us.

Just as we rejoice in the cross, the Lord rejoices over a spirit of repentance. "The LORD is nigh unto them that are of a broken heart; and saveth such as be of a contrite spirit" (Psalm 34:18). It is impossible to be saved without repentance. "Except ye repent, ye shall all likewise perish" (Luke 13:3).

To avoid water baptism is to ignore the witness of the Lord. The flood destroyed the world, but Noah and his family were saved by the water, because the water enabled the ark to float above the destruction. "The like figure whereunto even baptism doth also now save us" (I Peter 3:21).

While Adam was in a deep sleep, the Lord opened his side and from his rib made him a bride (Genesis 2:21-22). The second Adam, after passing into death, also had His side opened. From the blood and water out of His side He has formed His bride—the church (Revelation 21:9).

SPIRIT

The six momentous hours of the crucifixion exhibited many miraculous signs. All these miracles proved that Jesus Christ was the Son of God.

1. There was darkness from noon until three p.m. (Mark 15:33).

2. The veil of the temple was torn from top to bottom (Mark 15:38).

3. The earth quaked and the rocks were rent at His death (Matthew 27:51).

4. Many tombs were opened and many saints who had died arose after Christ's resurrection and entered into Jerusalem (Matthew 27:52-53).

The profound words of the dying Savior uttered during this climatic experience are equal in importance with the miraculous signs. The seven recorded sayings of Jesus on the cross reveal much about our great Savior.

1. Concerning His murderers He said, "Father, forgive them; for they know not what they do" (Luke 23:34).

2. To the repentant thief, he offered hope: "Verily I say unto thee, To day shalt thou be with me in paradise" (Luke 23:43).

3. He provided for His mother, speaking first to her and then to John. "Woman, behold thy son! . . .Behold thy mother!" (John 19:26-27).

4. "Eloi, Eloi, lama sabachthani? which is, being interpreted, My God, my God, why has thou forsaken me?" (Mark 15:34).

5. "I thirst" (John 19:28).

6. "It is finished" (John 19:30).

7. "Father, into thy hands I commend my spirit" (Luke 23:46).

Much could be said about each statement. To summarize briefly, the first three statements reached out to others with forgiveness, salvation and care. The other four dealt with His own anguish in the throes of death. The last statement made by Jesus is especially significant; last words are always important.

"Father, into thy hands I commend my spirit" (Luke 23:46). With this statement His heart stopped. What blood remained in His body rested still in His veins. His muscles relaxed. The warmth of His flesh ebbed away. There was no longer any pulse, for the Savior was dead. The flesh of Jesus had expressed its ultimate surrender to the will of God. It was a total yielding in obedience. This is the witness of Spirit as Jesus gave up His Spirit in the transition from life to death.

The yielding up of Jesus' Spirit is another witness to our spiritual birth. It was a spiritual transition. The Spirit left the flesh of Christ to return again at the resurrection.

Through His *death* we have *life*. By giving up His life, He provided the means for humanity to receive life in the place of death. By yielding up His Spirit in death, He made a way for us to receive His Holy Spirit and have new life.

Jesus told His disciples. "And I will pray the Father, and he shall give you another Comforter, that he may abide with you for ever; even the Spirit of truth. . . .I will not leave you comfortless: I will come to you" (John 14:16-18).

Because Jesus subjected Himself to the penalty of sin, which is death, we have been made free from sin and death (Romans 8:2). We are reconciled to God by the death of His son.

Romans 5 compares Jesus to Adam to illustrate this truth further. "For if by one man's offence death reigned by one; much more they which receive abundance of grace and of the gift of righteousness shall reign in life by one, Jesus Christ" (Romans 5:17).

There is nothing supernatural about dying. The death

127

of Jesus is the most convincing evidence of His humanity. His body responded in a very normal way to such abusive treatment. Yet when He spoke those last words, "Father, into thy hands I commend my spirit," supernatural phenomena occurred. Even though His death was natural, there was something supernatural about it.

The earth quaked and the rocks were rent as nature shuddered in anger at the spectacle of the Creator's death. The Savior had yielded up His Spirit, and nature growled in disapproval. At His resurrection many saints who were in their graves were raised from the dead and appeared in Jerusalem. So great was His victory that many received immediate power over death.

One of the greatest supernatural signs to accompany our Lord's death was the tearing of the Temple veil. At three in the afternoon the priests were preparing the evening sacrifice upon this solemn day. They were eyewitnesses to this marvelous symbolic occurrence. Suddenly, the thick, beautifully embroidered veil tore from top to bottom. If the priests had not been so blind, they would have known God was saying, "It's over! No more lamb's blood was necessary—no more Aaronic priesthood; no more bondage to the law and ordinances; and no more separation between humanity and the Shekinah."

Through the tearing of the flesh of Jesus, the veil of separation has been removed. "For he is our peace, who hath made both one, and hath broken down the middle wall of partition between us" (Ephesians 2:14).

In essence, the surrendering of the Lord's Spirit in death makes possible the filling of the Holy Ghost in every person who meets the conditions of repentence and faith.

"For the promise is unto you, and to your children, and to all that are afar off, even as many as the Lord our God shall call" (Acts 2:39).

He has united the Jew and Gentile into one church, ushering in a new and living way, making every born again believer a priest before God.

At the crucifixion of the Lord Jesus Christ we see a witness of the Spirit in the supernatural events that occurred as well as in His last words.

FOOTNOTES

[1]S. D. Gordon, *Quiet Talks with World Winners* (New York: Fleming H. Revell, 1908) p. 24.

[2]Copyright 1980 by Lanny Wolfe Music, a division of the Benson Company. Used by permission.

[3]Robert Coleman, *Written in Blood,* p. 100.

[4]Stuart Bergsma, M.D., "Did Jesus Die of a Broken Heart?" *The Calvin Forum,* March 1948, p. 165.

[5]*Ibid.*

9.

The New Testament Foundation As God's Witness

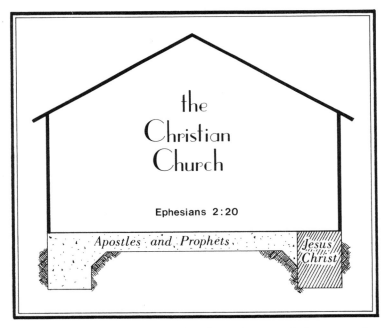

the Christian Church

Ephesians 2:20

Apostles and Prophets.

Jesus Christ

"And are built upon the foundation of the apostles and prophets, Jesus Christ himself being the chief corner stone" (Ephesians 2:20).

*T*here is a story about a foreman at a small town factory who blew the whistle each day at noon for lunch break. The city clock was in full view from the factory window. He would stand and watch the city clock until it struck 12:00 noon and then he would blow the whistle. The clerk at city hall would always check the old clock to make sure the hands were straight up when he heard the whistle blow. Of course, he was always pleased to see the old clock was right on time. Of course, neither the whistle nor the old city clock was reliable, for each was set by the other.

Official time in the United States is determined at the United States National Observatory in Washington, D.C. From this, standard time clocks across the country are set accordingly. Out of necessity, our government has established many uniform codes and standards for such things as weights and measurements, money, the calendar, industry and music. Without these standards, the country would be in disarray.

So it is with salvation. There are many different beliefs and concepts about salvation, but there is one standard. The Bible is our sole rule of faith. Everything must be measured by the Word of God. It is the final authority. Traditions will change, but God's Word will never change.

There is great security in acknowledging the centrality and supremacy of the Lord Jesus Christ and His Word, written by His apostles and prophets. This is the foundation of the New Testament Church (Ephesians 2:20). The life and teaching of Jesus and the actions and teaching of the Original Church form our foundation. Any belief not on that foundation will come to naught.

When reading and interpreting a biblical passage, it is important to discover the answer to three questions: Who wrote it? To whom was it written? For what purpose was it written? In considering these questions, it is clear that the New Testament consists of three major parts: the Gospels, the Acts of the Apostles, and the Epistles. The Gospels are the historical account of the life of the Lord Jesus Christ.

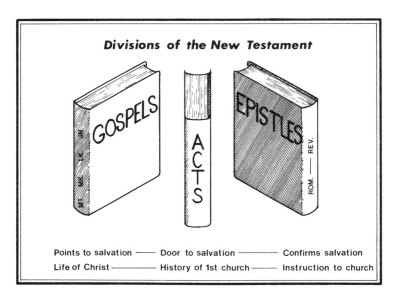

Divisions of the New Testament

Points to salvation —— Door to salvation ——— Confirms salvation		
Life of Christ———— History of 1st church—— Instruction to church		

The Acts of the Apostles is the historical record of the New Testament Church. This book recounts conversions from sin and false religions to Christianity. Here is the pattern for the Church. The Acts of the Apostles reveals what was required for new members to come into the church.

It is important to remember that the people in the time of the four Gospels were still living under the law of Moses. The New Testament church did not begin until the Day of Pentecost. The thief on the cross was among the last people to be saved under the law. By repenting of his sins, he was restored to his inheritance as a Jew under the old covenant, and Jesus was both his sacrifice and high priest.

The First Church was unique in that no member was raised by Christian parents. Every member was converted. The First Church had no "grandchildren" who were just presumed to be Christians because of their parents' status. Nor was anyone just absorbed into the church because of pedigree or influence. Certain demands were made on anyone who desired to become a Christian.

The birth of the First Church on the Day of Pentecost was remarkable (Acts 2). First of all, the city of Jerusalem was swelled with religious Jews from many parts of the world, and this gave the outpouring of the Holy Ghost great publicity. To the believers in the upper room, God gave an unforgettable miracle. The building filled with a sound like a rushing windstorm, and tongues like fire sat upon each believer. When the believers were filled with the Holy Ghost they began to speak in tongues (languages unknown to them). Their display of emotion and their tongues-speaking drew much attention. A crowd gathered, some mocking, others curious, and still others sincerely reaching out for God. How impressed people were to hear the disciples speaking in the tongues of the onlookers' native lands as they worshiped God. Many in the crowd were puzzled and some mocked, accusing the disciples of drunkenness. After Peter preached to the gathered crowd, 3000 people were added to the Christian church.

It is important to learn exactly what happened to these first converts, for they are our example and pattern. The 3000 converts at Pentecost repented of their sins, were baptized in the name of Jesus Christ, and received the baptism of the Holy Ghost. This is certain because Peter responded to their question of "What shall we do?" by saying, "Repent, and be baptized every one of you in the name of Jesus Christ for the remission of sins, and ye shall receive the gift of the Holy Ghost" (Acts 2:37-38). It is ludicrous to assume the apostles were so desperate for a big number that they counted people who did not obey exactly what Peter had just instructed them to do.

KEYS OF THE KINGDOM

That Peter was the spokesman at Pentecost has great significance. All the twelve apostles were chosen and trained by Jesus to be the foundation of the church, but Peter had a special role to play as the first spokesman.

After Peter's bold confession of the identity of Jesus—"Thou art the Christ, the Son of the living God"—Jesus proclaimed, "Thou art Peter, and upon this rock I will build my church; and the gates of hell shall not prevail against it. And I will give unto thee the keys of the kingdom of heaven: and whatsoever thou shalt bind on earth shall be bound in heaven: and whatsoever thou shalt loose on earth shall be loosed in heaven" (Matthew 16:16, 18-19).

This was not authority to stand in heaven and unlock the pearly gates but authority to open the door of heaven by preaching the message of salvation. Peter was not given the position of *judgment* but of *proclamation*. The Book of Acts describes how Peter fulfilled this role. Peter was the one who proclaimed the gospel message to the three races of people in the Apostolic Age.

1. *Jews.* The Jews were descendants of Abraham. They were not only a racial group but a religious group as well. The first Christians were Jews who accepted the gospel (Romans 1:16). Peter was the first to preach the gospel to the Jews. This occurred on the Day of Pentecost, the birthday of the New Testament church (Acts 2:14). After preaching about Christ's death, burial and resurrection, he instructed them to repent, be baptized in Jesus' name and receive the Holy Ghost.

2. *Samaritans.* After Assyria conquered the ten-tribe nation of Israel in Old Testament times, they took many Israelites into captivity. The remnant that they left behind intermarried with settlers from Mesopotamia and other areas, producing a mixed race. The Samaritans, as they became known, developed their own religion based on Judaism, yet unique in many ways. They were not Gentiles, strictly speaking, because of their Jewish blood, yet the Jews detested them because of their mixed racial and religious heritage.

Philip the evangelist went to Samaria and preached the gospel (Acts 8:5). He had great results—of healings, casting out of demons and water baptisms—but not until Peter and John came to Samaria did anyone receive the Holy Ghost. "They sent unto them Peter and John: who, when they were come down, prayed for them, that they might receive the Holy Ghost: (For as yet he was fallen upon none of them: only they were baptized in the name of the Lord Jesus.) Then laid they their hands on them, and they received the Holy Ghost" (Acts 8:14-17). We should note that Peter was instrumental in opening the door of salvation to the Samaritans.

3. *Gentiles.* This included everybody who was not a Jew or a Samaritan. The gospel reached this group of people in Acts 10. Once again, God used Peter to open the door of salvation to this new group. At God's direction, he went to the house of Cornelius and preached the gospel to the Gentiles for the first time. Cornelius was an Italian centurion—a captain over one hundred men in the Roman army. While Peter was still preaching to the people gathered in his house, they received the Holy Ghost with the evidence of speaking in tongues after which they were baptized in Jesus' name (Acts 10:44-48).

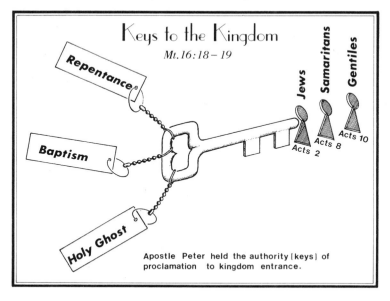

Keys to the Kingdom
Mt. 16:18-19

Repentance

Baptism

Holy Ghost

Jews — Acts 2
Samaritans — Acts 8
Gentiles — Acts 10

Apostle Peter held the authority [keys] of proclamation to kingdom entrance.

Peter's gospel message was threefold: repentance, water baptism and the Holy Ghost with the evidence of speaking in tongues. It is most succinctly stated in Acts 2:38. Let us study each of these cardinal doctrines of salvation.

REPENTANCE

Repentance is a fundamental teaching throughout the Word of God as the following points show.

1. *Old Testament.* A common Hebrew verb *shub* is used to mean to turn from sin and evil to God and righteousness. "In this usage, the word means not merely to change the direction, but to turn right around and face in the opposite way."[1] The prophets of the Old Testament preached that the ceremonial law was insufficent without moral obedience. God has always required repentance and commitment from His people. "If my people, which are called by my name, shall humble themselves, and pray, and seek my face, and turn from their wicked ways; then will I hear from heaven, and will forgive their sin, and will heal their land" (II Chronicles 7:14). David's prayer in Psalm 51 is a beautiful example of repentance.

2. *John the Baptist.* The focus of John's message was, "Repent ye: for the kingdom of heaven is at hand" (Matthew 3:2). He challenged men to forsake worldly living in order to qualify for entrance into the kingdom of God. They were to bring forth fruits worthy of repentance. The essence of John's message was repentance. It became the foundation upon which Jesus launched His ministry.

3. *Jesus Christ.* At Jesus' first appearance in Galilee after John's imprisonment, He preached, "The time is fulfilled, and the kingdom of God is at hand: repent ye, and believe the gospel" (Mark 1:15). Jesus summed up the pur-

pose of His mission by saying, "I am not come to call the righteous, but sinners to repentance" (Matthew 9:13). The parables of the lost sheep, the lost coin, and the lost son remind us of the joy in heaven over one sinner who repents (Luke 15:7). Jesus warned, "Except ye repent, ye shall all likewise perish" (Luke 13:5).

The whole ministry of Jesus can be described as a ministry of repentance. His last words to His apostles explain the purpose of His death, burial and resurrection: "That repentance and remission of sins should be preached in his name among all nations" (Luke 24:47).

4. *New Testament Church.* On the first day of the church, in the first message preached by the church, Peter's first command was to repent (Acts 2:38). Repentance is a central requirement throughout the New Testament, not only initially at conversion, but also as a permanent attitude and lifestyle. Here are examples of a direct injunction to repent:

    (a) Peter to the Jews at Pentecost (Acts 2:38).
    (b) Peter to those gathered at Solomon's Porch (Acts 3:19).
    (c) Peter to Simon the Sorcerer (Acts 8:22).
    (d) Paul to the Athenians at Mars' Hill (Acts 17:30).
    (e) Paul to the Gentiles (Acts 26:20).

It is important to understand the relationship between initial faith and repentance. Repentance without faith is powerless and actually impossible. One theologian wrote, "Faith and repentance are two sides of one and the same spiritual process. If faith be the act of the soul in turning to God in Christ, repentance is the same act viewed as the soul turning away from sin."[2] Actually saving faith encompasses more than repentance, but the preceding quota-

140

tion does contain a valid point. Faith is positive, looking forward to life in God's kingdom. Repentance is turning our back on past sinfulness. One is incomplete without the other.

BAPTISM

The law of Moses instituted washing as part of various purification ceremonies. Washing in water was also required of Jewish proselytes after circumcision. It represented purification or washing from pagan impurity. This Jewish custom was not necessarily a prototype of New Testament baptism, but historically it served as an introduction to the New Testament practice.

John the Baptist's baptism was not just a Levitical washing, but it signified a spiritual turning away from sins and entry into a purer life. His baptism unto repentance was a prelude to Christian baptism in the name of Jesus Christ.

Christian baptism was not just a carry-over from Jewish proselyte baptism or from John's baptism. All converts to Christianity were baptized in the name of Jesus Christ to show their new allegiance to Him and as part of entrance into His church. Jewish, Samaritan and Gentiles converts were all baptized in the name of Jesus. John's disciples in Acts 19 were rebaptized in the name of Jesus, signifying the superiority and importance of Christian baptism.

The following charts summarize the scriptural practice and teaching concerning water baptism.

Baptism By Example in the New Testament Church

Text	Agent	Believers	Location	Formula	Mode	Purpose
Acts 2:38-41	Peter	3000 Jews	Jerusalem	name of Jesus Christ	●	remission of sins
Acts 8:12,16	Philip	all believers	Samaria	name of the Lord Jesus	●	●
Acts 9:18; 22:16	Ananias	Saul	Damascus	name of the Lord	immersion (Romans 6:4)	wash away sins
Acts 10:48	Peter	Cornelius & household	Caesarea	name of the Lord	●	salvation (Acts 11:14)
Acts 19:5	Paul	12 disciples of John	Ephesus	name of the Lord Jesus	●	●
Acts 16:33	Paul & Silas	Jailer & household	Philippi	●	●	●
Acts 16:15	Paul & Silas	Lydia	Philippi	●	●	●
Acts 8:38	Philip	Ethiopian eunuch	Gaza	●	immersion	●
Acts 18:8	Paul	many Corinthians	Corinth	name of Christ (I Corinthians 1:12-13)	●	●

● NOT STATED

John's Baptism By Example

TEXT	BELIEVERS	LOCATION	FORMULA	MODE	PURPOSE
Matthew 3:6,11 Mark 1:4-5	of Jerusalem, of Judea, around Jordan	Jordan River	unto repentance	with water	remission of sins
Luke 3:3,12-14	publicans & soldiers	Jordan River	repentance (Acts 13:24)	water (Acts 1:5; 11:16)	remission of sins
Matthew 3:13-16	Jesus	Jordan River	●	immersion	to fulfill all righteousness
John 3:22-24	●	Aenon	repentance (Acts 19:4)	by much water	●

● NOT STATED

142

New Testament Teaching On Water Baptism					
SPEAKER	TEXT	TO WHOM	FORMULA	MODE	PURPOSE
Jesus	Mark 16:16	the eleven	●	●	salvation
Jesus	Matthew 28:19	the eleven	name of Father, Son & Holy Ghost	●	●
Jesus	John 3:3 - 5	Nicodemus	●	born of water	enter kingdom of God
Paul	I Corinthians 10:1 - 4	Corinthians	●	in the sea	typology
Peter	I Peter 3:20-21	elect of God	●	by water	salvation
Paul	Romans 6:3 - 5	Romans	into Jesus Christ	immersion	to be resurrected
Paul	Galatians 3:27	Galatians	into Christ	●	put on Christ
Paul	Colossians 2:11 -12	Colossians	●	immersion	to be resurrected
Paul	Titus 3:5	Titus	●	washing	salvation
Paul	Hebrew 6:1-2	Hebrews	●	●	a principle of doctrine

● NOT STATED

The New Testament Church baptized adults by immersion in water in the name of Jesus Christ.

BAPTISM IN THE HOLY GHOST

Peter declared on the Day of Pentecost that the outpouring of the Holy Ghost was the fulfillment of Joel's prophecy (Acts 2:16-21). Pentecost was a day of fulfillment of other prophecies as well, including the following.

1. Joel 2:28: "I will pour out my spirit upon all flesh."
2. Ezekiel 36:27: "And I will put my spirit within you."
3. Isaiah 28:11: "For with stammering lips and another

143

tongue will he speak to this people."

4. Jeremiah 31:33: " I will put my law in their inward parts, and write it in their hearts."

5. John the Baptist (Matthew 3:11): "He shall baptize you with the Holy Ghost, and with fire."

6. Jesus Christ (Luke 24:49): "I send the promise of my Father upon you: but tarry ye in the city of Jerusalem, until ye be endued with power from on high."

In the Old Testament, the Holy Ghost rested upon and anointed a few people for certain purposes. But the promised outpouring is an abiding experience available to all flesh.

Speaking in tongues is the initial sign of the baptism of the Holy Ghost. This is evident from a consideration of the five places in the New Testament where believers received the baptism of the Holy Ghost. In each case it is apparent that the initial sign was speaking in tongues.

1. Pentecost (Acts 2:4): "And they were all filled with the Holy Ghost, and began to speak with other tongues, as the Spirit gave them utterance."

2. Cornelius and his household (Acts 10:45-46): "On the Gentiles also was poured out the gift of the Holy Ghost. For they heard them speak with tongues, and magnify God."

3. Disciples of John the Baptist (Acts 19:6): "The Holy Ghost came on them; and they spake with tongues, and prophesied."

4. Apostle Paul's conversion (Acts 9:17): This verse does not describe how Paul received the Holy Ghost or mention that he spoke in tongues, but later he said, "I thank my God, I speak with tongues more than ye all" (I Corinthians 14:18).

5. Believers at Samaria (Acts 8:17-19): Simon had seen healings, baptisms, and exorcisms. When he saw people filled with the Holy Ghost by the laying on of hands, he offered money to purchase that kind of power. Something definite and miraculous happened to the people when they were baptized in the Holy Ghost.

Some believe the baptism in the Holy Ghost is an experience subsequent to conversion. They think it is an optional experience for extra power, like a spare tire in the trunk of a car. It is not necessary, they say, but nice to have. One proponent of this belief has stated, "For a person planning to die within the next few days, there probably aren't any great advantages to receiving the Baptism in the Holy Spirit. But for those who don't plan to leave this vale of problems soon, there are tremendous advantages."[3] This position is not scriptural, as the following discussion will show.

In analyzing this position, it is important to remember that the dispensation or age of the law did not end until Jesus was crucified. The new covenant could not become effective until after the death, burial and resurrection of Jesus (See John 7:39; 16:7; Hebrews 9:14-17.) The events described in the four Gospels occurred under the law. It is incorrect to go here to find examples of entrance into the New Testament church. Obviously, before Pentecost no one received the baptism in the Holy Ghost. Yet people were saved under the law as they waited for the new covenent.

During this transition of ages, there was an interim period from the ministry of John the Baptist until Pentecost. This four-year period included the ministry of John the Baptist and Jesus Christ simultaneously. Converts complied with the message of obedient faith and repentance and continued to live by the law.

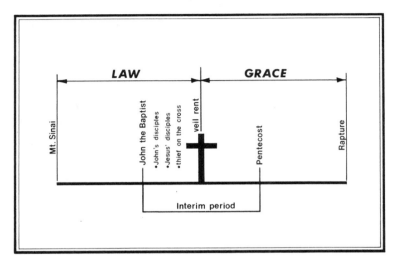

Since we are still living in the New Testament church age, often called the dispensation of grace, which began on the Day of Pentecost, we know the baptism in the Holy Ghost is still available today (Acts 2:39).

No distinction is made in the Scriptures between faith at conversion and the baptism in the Holy Ghost. New Testament converts received this wonderful gift at the time of conversion. There is no record of a dichotomy of experience, whereby they were saved at one time and received the Holy Ghost at another time.

Some passages state in very simple terms the direction to salvation. "For God so loved the world, that he gave his only begotten Son, that whosoever believeth in him should not perish, but have everlasting life" (John 3:16).

146

Paul instructed the Philippian jailer, who was about to commit suicide, "Believe on the Lord Jesus Christ, and thou shalt be saved, and thy house" (Acts 16:31). These verses state that faith in Jesus Christ brings salvation, that such faith is the fundamental means by which a person is saved. This is an accurate summary of the gospel message in its most concentrated form.

If a person were to ask the question, "How do you get from New York City to Los Angeles?" a truthful answer would be "Go west." Those two words are accurate enough to get him started in the right direction. But it is unlikely that he would reach his destination without further direction. Similarly, while faith in Jesus Christ and His redemptive work is the way to salvation, for a person to experience salvation he must learn how to exercise saving faith through obedience to the gospel message. Salvation by faith means more than mental assent and acknowledgement of Jesus as personal Savior. The following questions reveal that active obedience to Christ's gospel is necessary to saving faith.

1. Is verbal confession necessary? "If thou shalt confess with thy mouth the Lord Jesus, and shalt believe in thine heart that God hath raised him from the dead, thou shalt be saved" (Romans 10:9). Obviously, a silent mental prayer is incomplete. "With the mouth confession is made unto salvation" (Romans 10:10).

2. Must Jesus be only acknowledged as Savior? According to Romans 10:9 we must also acknowledge Him as Lord, and for this confession to be truthful we must obey Him. Making Him "Lord" involves repentance. It is a commitment to discipleship, a decision to change from a life of sin to a life pleasing to God. "Except ye repent, ye shall

147

all likewise perish" (Luke 13:3). "Repent ye therefore, and be converted, that your sins may be blotted out" (Acts 3:19).

3. Is baptism necssary? "He that believeth and is baptized shall be saved" (Mark 16:16). "The like figure whereunto even baptism doth also now save us" (I Peter 3:21). (See also Acts 2:38; 22:16; Romans 6:3-4; Galatians 3:27; Colossians 2:11-12.)

4. Is the baptism of the Holy Ghost necessary? "Except a man be born of water and of the Spirit, he cannot enter into the kingdom of God" (John 3:5). "Now if any man have not the Spirit of Christ, he is none of his" (Romans 8:9). (See also Acts 2:38; Acts 11:12-18; Romans 8:16; I Corinthians 12:13; Colossians 1:27; and Titus 3:5.)

FOOTNOTES

[1]James Hastings, ed., "Repentance," *Encylopedia of Religion and Ethics,* (New York: Charles Scribner's Sons, 1908-22), X, 731.
[2]*Ibid.,* p. 733.
[3]Jimmy Swaggart, *The Baptism in the Holy Ghost* (Baton Rouge: Jimmy Swaggart Ministries), p. 12.

10.

History As A Witness

A panoramic view of Christianity shows a church with periods of stagnation and decay, but with times of revival and renewal. Decline came during times of acceptance and good will. Revival often came during times of opposition and persecution. True revival has come when people returned to the Apostolic Church of the first century as a pattern and standard by which to measure all truth of doctrine and practice.

Hints of decline in the church can be seen in the last book of the Bible, "The Revelation of Jesus Christ." Jesus rebuked many of the churches for their growing decline in doctrine and spiritual fervor (Revelation 2-3). Church historian Lars Qualbon has described the continued spiritual decline in the second century:

> *The enthusiastic prophetic element in early Christian life was gradually being replaced by a growing formalism in teaching and in worship. . . . The specially "gifted" became fewer and their prophecies perhaps less reliable; the expectation of the speedy return of the Lord was no longer so general; a new generation had grown up that had not been won directly for the Church from heathenism, but had been born and educated in Christian homes. Instead of the immediate gifts of the Spirit, Christians rather relied on organizations and out-*

ward religious authority.[1]

This chapter traces the practice of repentance, water baptism, and the baptism of the Holy Ghost throughout church history.

REPENTANCE

Times of Persecution

Severe persecution began in the first century under Nero (A.D. 54-68), who falsely accused the Christians of setting fire to Rome. The apostles all died by martyrdom except John. The emperors of Rome continued to persecute the church for many years. Not until Constantine became emperor did the Christian church find any lasting relief from persecution.

There were many sincere Christians during this period. Many gave their lives for their faith. Although many false doctrines arose, for the most part converts experienced genuine repentance. Deep commitment was required in the face of such opposition. Many converts were won because of the spirit of bravery displayed by Christian martyrs. Those who converted to Christianity certainly had to demonstrate a strong decision of loyalty.

The Apostles' Creed

This creed developed from late second century baptismal creeds; it was not composed by the Apostles. It was a statement of faith required of new converts before baptism in water. The earliest exact text dates from about A.D. 400. The following is the creed required to be read or memorized by new converts:

I believe in God almighty (the Father almighty)
And in Christ Jesus, his only Son, our Lord
Who was born of the Holy Spirit and the Virgin Mary
Who was crucified under Pontius Pilate and was
    buried
And the third day rose from the dead
Who ascended into heaven
And sits on the right hand of the Father
Whence he comes to judge the living and the dead
And in the Holy Ghost
The holy church
The remission of sins
The resurrection of the flesh
The life everlasting.

Even though the church fathers had good intentions, they began a trend toward formalism. They began to emphasize theological adherence over real heart-felt love for and commitment to the Lord Jesus Christ, which is the essence of true repentance.

The Edict of Milan

In the city of Milan, Constantine issued an edict in the year 313 that made Christianity legal. The church had suffered persecution since its birth. This edict stopped the persecution and proclaimed freedom of conscience. Constantine professed to forsake the sun-god Mithra and embrace Christianity. He gave large sums of money to the church and built many magnificent church buildings. The Roman army replaced their emblem of an eagle with a cross. It was no longer shameful to be a Christian, but an honor. As a result, thousands upon thousands of pagans joined the church. Many were Christians in name only. The requirements of conversion became watered down. Repentance became a lost experience in this large numerical growth of the institutional church. Infant baptism became a common practice, eliminating the conversion experience completely for those born in the church.

Fall of the Roman Empire in 476

The fall of the Roman Empire actually strengthened the church in power and influence, but caused it to deteriorate even further spiritually. The Teutonic barbarians who destroyed the empire infused the Catholic Church. Many of them were already Arian Christians. Although baptism was still a part of conversion, it was just a ritualistic formality. The church became glutted with large numbers of unconverted heathenish people. Repentance was certainly not required of new converts.

The Dark Ages (590-1294)

Gross corruption permeated the Catholic Church during this period. Great power struggles existed between the Roman bishops and the Greek bishops until the church finally split. The popes of Rome became so powerful and wealthy that they frequently dominated the kings of Europe. The church bore no resemblance to the Apostolic Church of the first century. The church became more concerned about people's allegience to the authority of the church than to the Lord. The church was no longer persecuted, but it began to practice its own persecution. It was a very dark hour.

Reformation

The Reformation was a movement that cried out against many extra biblical elements of Catholicism. John Wyclif, John Hus and Savonarola were forerunners of the Reformation. Martin Luther is credited with starting the Reformation in 1517 by posting the ninety-five thesis against false doctrines and practices. For the most part, the Reformers were preoccupied by their differences with the Roman Church and sought to reform the traditional church structure.

Tertullian in the third century, had defined repentance as an "emotion of disgust" at some previously cherished sin. Over time, the Catholic Church placed emphasis on the negative emotion of remorse, and its doctrine of penance began to confuse the real meaning of repentance. One writer has explained the Catholic doctrine and the Protestant reaction:

> *This doctrine is that repentance is only part of the sacrament of penance, the two other elements being confession and satisfaction. The Reformers went back to the New Testament idea. Luther's doctrine was that repentance consisted of sorrow for sin and faith in Christ. He maintained that the whole life should be a penitential act. The Reformation started as a protest against false or inadequate conceptions of repentance.*[2]

A sixteenth century group called the Anabaptists were more radical in their attempt to reform. They held that Christians should adopt the lifestyle of discipleship: "The Christian's relationship with Jesus Christ must go beyond

155

inner experience and acceptance of doctrines. It must involve a daily walk with God, in which Christ's teaching and example shapes a transformed style of life."[3]

Revival in the 1600's and 1700's

George Fox and the Quakers, in England, along with the Pietists in Continental Europe, rejected the sterile religion of the seventeenth century. "Pietism taught that the regeneration of man took place, not in baptism, but in a specific experience of conversion."[4] The Pietists believed that Christianity was a lifestyle and that every believer could have an inner religious experience.

In the eighteenth century, the Wesley brothers preached in Europe and America. They taught that being a Christian involved a definite *method* of lifestyle. Thus they became known as "Methodists." George Whitefield of England preached with the Wesley brothers. "Whitefield had been preaching on the necessity of biblical conversion and spiritual regeneration as opposed to baptismal regeneration. This won for him great hostility among the Anglicans, who closed their pulpits to him, forcing him to take up open air preaching."[5]

Revival in the 1800's

Charles Finney (1792-1875) conducted great revival campaigns in America. During a time when Calvinism had stifled the vitality of the churches, "he appealed to men to respond to the grace of God in repentance and faith."[6] This emphasis upon the need to make a commitment to God in repentance has continued to be one of the basic beliefs in conservative Protestant churches.

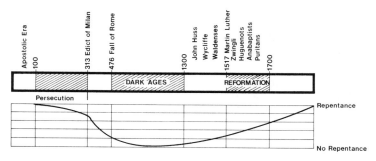

Repentance in History

BAPTISM

Christian baptism has been practiced throughout history with a variety of methods and motives. The subject is a vast one and difficult to address in a brief way. We will deal with the matter under three separate subjects: meaning, mode, and formula.

Baptism: Its Meaning

"In the primitive community, . . .baptism is universally practiced as a rite of admission into the Christian community."[7] "As the sacrament of admission, baptism always stood till the religious divisions of post-Reformation days. It so stands for the vast majority of Christians at present."[8]

The First Church did not believe that water baptism was merely a symbol of a prior spiritual work in them; they taught that God actually remitted sins at water baptism. This belief continued into the second century, but with some distortion.

To Hermas (115-140), baptism was the very foundation of the church, which is "builded upon

157

waters." Even to the philosophical Justin (153)
baptism affected "regeneration" and "illumination."
In Tertullian's estimate, it conveyed eternal life
itself.[9]

It appears that as the experience of the Holy Ghost baptism began to wane, the ceremony of water baptism came to be viewed as the source of regeneration.

The doctrine of original sin developed, which held that everyone was born not only with an innate nature to sin but also with actual guilt for sin, which could only be removed by water baptism. This doctrine, along with the high mortality rate among infants, brought about the practice of infant baptism. "The first mention of infant baptism, and an obscure one, was about 185, by Irenaeus."[10] Baptism took on a mystical characteristic with attention being placed upon the act itself instead of on the attitude and faith of the one being baptized.

Many elaborate regulations developed as a result of this theological interpretation of baptism:

Even before Nicaea (A.D. 325), the ceremon-
ies attendant upon adult baptism were increasingly
elaborated to include fasting and prayer before the
rite, a vigil all the preceding night, renunciation of
the devil at dawn, anointing the body against the
devil, the actual immersion with first recitation of
the baptismal confession, clothing with white gar-
ments, laying on of hands, signing with the cross
in oil of chrism, acceptance by the bishop for the
community, first participation in the Eucharist, and
partaking of milk and honey.[11]

Augustine (A.D. 354-430) taught that water baptism was the vehicle of entrance into the body of Christ. He held that both original sin and actual sins were removed at the time of baptism. This doctrine helped make infant baptism a normal practice. The belief was that it provided the child protection from original sin as well as continued protection from evil influences, allowing him to grow to maturity.

Baptism during the medieval period did not change in practice or theory. "The ritual was modified here and there in the various countries, but is preserved everywhere in its essential points."[12] Baptism was considered to confer an indelible character, which included the marks of Christ. Only two exceptions were made in the necessity of baptism. First was the baptism by blood. This was death as a martyr. Second was baptism by desire. This made provision for those who desired to be baptized but because of peril or some extenuating circumstance could not. Their desire to be baptized was sufficient.

At the Council of Trent in 1546 the Roman Church stated that original sin can only be removed by the merit of Jesus Christ, which is by the Church in baptism. In an effort to resist the Reformation, this council explicitly stated that baptism outside the Roman Church was invalid.

The Reformation resulted in many modifications in the traditional doctrine of baptism. Here is a summary of the beliefs of three of the most famous Reformers.

1. *Martin Luther* believed baptism was necessary, but he said no sacrament, including baptism, was valid without faith. This view would seemingly exclude infant baptism, yet Luther insisted on the efficacy of infant baptism based on the faith of the sponsors. Later he changed his view

to hold that infants themselves believed by faith God gave them. This concept was based on his belief in the doctrine of individual predestination.

2. *Ulrich Zwingli* believed baptism was an outward sign of grace already the possession of the believer. Baptism was only a sign or ceremony of true reality.

3. *John Calvin* placed more stress upon baptism than Zwingli. For him "Baptism is the seal upon election and the solemn sign by which those who already belong to Christ's body are received into the church."[13] He did not favor baptism of infants, but his followers continued the practice.

The Anabaptists made radical changes in the traditional baptismal practices. "All rejected infant baptism and practiced the baptism of adults upon confession of faith."[14] Those who were baptized as infants were rebaptized. They were greatly persecuted by the Catholic Church as well as by the Reformers.

The rise of rationalism affected the importance put upon baptism. "In everyday language, rationalism means that everything is judged by reason. Bound up with this is the idea that, when this is done, belief in God and the supernatural will be swept away; we shall be left with nature and hard facts."[15] This belief removed the doctrine of original sin and eliminated the need for divine grace. Baptism became an outward rite signifying adherence to the church rather than a means of forgiveness and regeneration.

George Fox and the Quakers rejected baptism altogether, emphasizing inward regeneration without outward ceremony. Revivals in the nineteenth century gave baptism a deeper meaning. Baptism became the rite which

160

incorporated the believer into church life.

In the twentieth century, Oneness Pentecostals returned to the biblical teaching that baptism is part of the new birth and is for the remission of sins.

Baptism: Its Mode

By mode we mean the physical mechanics of the act, particularly the practices of sprinkling or pouring versus immersion.

As discussed in previous chapters, baptism in the Apostolic Church was by immersion. Immersion continued to be the method of baptism into the second century. "Early Christians practiced immersion, or submerging a person in water, as a method of baptism."[16] For further historical evidence, see Lewis Manuwal, *Water Baptism According to the Bible and Historical References.*

The first real evidence of the practice of sprinkling is in the third century. "Pictures in the catacombs would seem to indicate that the submersion was not always complete."[17] Cyprian, a church father from Africa, defended baptism by pouring, but "immersion continued as the prevailing practice until the late Middle Ages in the West; in the East it so remains."[18]

In the third century, a number of elaborate rituals developed around baptism. Purity before baptism was deemed so important that sometimes three years of preparation were required. Hippolytus's account of baptism at Rome involved a question-and-answer dialogue between the convert and the baptizer. Three questions of faith were asked. After answering "I believe," the convert was baptized after each question, going down into the water three times. The *Didache* taught that a person was to be immersed three times, in the name of the Father, Son, and Holy Spirit. Sprinkling was permitted where there was insufficient water for immersion.

"When the church spread to colder countries, baptism by pouring (or affusion) became common, at least as an alternative mode of administration."[19] Infant baptism also helped to make affusion more popular.

During the Middle Ages, according to Thomas Aquinas, immersion was still the most common method of baptism. It also had the approval of this great scholastic theologian.

The convenience of sprinkling made it popular in the Catholic Church. It was a widespread practice at the time of the Reformation. Martin Luther preferred immersion as more true to the original practice, but his followers retained sprinkling."[20]

John Smyth, after being convinced against infant baptism by Mennonites, baptized himself by pouring in 1608. He was the father of the Baptist movement. Even though he was baptized by pouring, the Baptists soon began to baptize by immersion. Most Evangelicals today practice baptism by immersion.

The Roman Catholic Church usually baptizes by sprinkling or pouring. "Baptism is validly administered whether performed by total immersion, by infusion, or by aspersion. By infusion, the water is poured on the head, forehead, or face. The water must flow on the skin of the person being baptized, not merely on the hair. By aspersion, water is sprinkled on the head."[21]

Baptism: Its Formula
By formula we mean the actual verbal wording used

by the baptizer at the time of the rite, particularly the use of the name of Jesus Christ versus the Trinitarian formula of Father, Son and Holy Ghost.

According to the New Testament, the Apostolic Church baptized in the name of Jesus Christ. The early post-apostolic church did also. Everywhere in the oldest sources it is stated that baptism takes place "in the name of Jesus."[22] The following references confirm this fact.

1. *The Interpreter's Dictionary of the Bible* (New York: Abingdon, 1962, I, 351: "The evidence. . .suggests that baptism in early Christianity was administered, not in the threefold name, but 'in the name of Jesus Christ' or 'in the name of the Lord Jesus.' "

2. *A Dictionary of Christ and the Gospels* (New York: Abingdon, 1909), I, 170: "The essential feature of Baptism was its marking the union of the soul to Christ, and therefore, it sufficed to call it 'Baptism into the name of the Lord Jesus.' "

3. *Eerdman's Handbook of the History of Christianity* (Grand Rapids: Eerdmans, 1977), p. 123: "Paul objected to their abuse and misunderstanding. Baptism should be in the name of Jesus. . . .'In the name of Jesus' meant that the new converts passed under his authority, and confessed him as Lord."

4. *Encyclopedia of Religions* ed. Maurice Canney (1970) p. 53: "Persons were baptized at first 'in the name of Jesus Christ' (Acts 2:38; 10:48) or 'in the name of the Lord Jesus' (Acts 8:16; 19:5). Afterwards, with the development of the doctrine of the Trinity, they were baptized 'in the name of the Father and of the Son and of the Holy Ghost.' "

5. *Encyclopedia of Religion and Ethics,* ed. James

163

Hastings (1937), II, 378: The church "sealed the reception of the candidate into the holy community by invoking 'the fair name' of the Lord Jesus upon his head."

6. *The New Schaff-Herzog Religious Encyclopedia of Religious Knowledge* (1957), I, 435: "The New Testament knows only baptism in the name of Jesus."

7. *Dictionary of Church History,* ed. Jerald Braver, p. 32: "The full Trinitarian formula did not emerge until the 2nd. century."

8. *Dictionary of the Bible,* ed. James Hastings (1937), p. 83: "It must be acknowledged that the formula of the threefold name. . .does not appear to have been employed by the primitive Church, which, so far as our information goes, baptized 'in' or 'into the name of Jesus' or 'Jesus Christ' or 'the Lord Jesus.' "

9. *The International Standard Bible Encyclopedia,* ed. Geoffrey Bromiley (1979), I. p. 421: "In every account of the performance of the rite in apostolic times a much shorter formula is used [shorter than the Trinitarian formula]. The three thousand believers were baptized on the day of Pentecost 'in the name of Jesus' (Acts 2:38); and the same formula was used at the baptism of Cornelius and those who were with him (10:48)."

10. *Encyclopedia of Theology,* ed. Karl Raher (1975), p. 67: "But after the glorification of the Lord the apostles administered the traditional rite in a new way and with a new import; they now baptized in the name of Jesus, that is, in accordance with the gospel in the name of Jesus, assigning men to him, invoking his name over the candidate."

11. *A Dictionary of Christian Theology,* ed. Alan Richardson (1969), p. 172: "In the earliest days of the

Church, it appears that baptism was often administered 'in the name of Christ.' "

In the second century, the use of Father, Son and Holy Ghost began. It is interesting to note that baptism in a Trinitarian-style formula was apparently practiced before the Trinity became a doctrine of the Church. Tertullian (A.D. 150-225) was the first writer to use the term *Trinity.* He introduced the Trinitarian terminology used later in the development of the doctrine. At the Council of Nicea (A.D. 325), church leaders began the formal development of Trinity as an official doctrine of the Catholic Church. "It was not until the Council of Constantinople in 381. . .that the modern doctrine of the trinity gained permanent victory."[23]

Those who began baptizing in the threefold formula apparently did so on the basis of Matthew 28:19. They repeated the words of Jesus instead of understanding and obeying the command as did the Apostolic Church. "There is no mention of baptism in the name of the Trinity in the New Testament, except in the command attributed to Christ in Matthew 28:19."[24]

Cyril of Jerusalem (died A.D. 444) described the ceremony of baptism during his day. After much preparation, involving fasting, renouncing Satan, confession of the creed and anointing with oil, the actual baptism took place: "Each makes answer to the threefold question, if he believes in the Father, Son and Holy Ghost, with the prescribed formula and is submerged at each confession, three times therefore."[25]

Since the doctrine of the Trinity was adopted and gained dominance in Christendom, most churches have used the formula of Father, Son and Holy Ghost without question. The formula in baptism was not an issue for the Reformers. There is historical evidence for the practice of baptism in Jesus' name among various groups in later church history, but it has been primarily the Oneness Pentecostals who have returned to the apostolic formula.

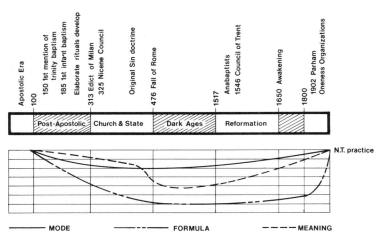

Baptism in History

BAPTISM IN THE HOLY GHOST

The phrase "baptism in the Holy Ghost" comes from John the Baptist's prophecy that the Messiah would baptize with the Holy Ghost and fire (Matthew 3:11). Also, just before his ascension, Jesus said, "Ye shall be baptized with the Holy Ghost not many days hence" (Acts 1:5).

Believers in the Apostolic Church spoke with tongues as the Spirit gave them utterance when they were filled or baptized with the Holy Ghost. Tongues-speaking continued to be a practice in the early post-apostolic church, not only at the initial filling, but also as a manifested gift of the Spirit.

This section reviews the phenomenon of speaking in tongues (glossolalia) from the close of the Apostolic Age until the present. Periods of silence on the subject of tongues can be interpreted in many ways: (1) Early-church fathers wrote primarily against opponents. If tongues-speaking was universally accepted and practiced, it might not be mentioned. (2) In later times, records could have been destroyed, particularly by opponents. (3) Few or none spoke in tongues at that time. (4) People did not recognize its significance and therefore did not write about it.

The Montanists

In the second century, it is recorded that a group called the Montanists spoke in tongues. Their founder and prophet, Montanus, believed he was the mouthpiece of the Holy Ghost. They were labeled as heretics and fanatics by their opponents and excommunicated by early synods of bishops. Their visions, prophecies, and intense religious excitement created suspicion. The most distinguished Montanist was Tertullian. His treatise, *Against Marcion,* challenged the heretic Marcion to display the interpretation of tongues as a sign that his church was true.

Irenaeus

Irenaeus was a church father who had known Polycarp. He was the Bishop of Lyons in Gaul during the last quarter of the second century. He referred to tongues-speaking three times. The first mention is a reference to its occurrence at Pentecost. In the second mention, he described tongues as speaking in foreign languages. His third mention reveals that tongues-speaking was practiced in his day and favorably declares it to reveal the mysteries of God.

Chrysostom and Augustine

"The combined evidence of Chrysostom and Augustine would indicate that tongue speaking had passed off the scene by the late fourth century in both East and West."[26] They both indicated they had no firsthand experience with the phenomenon, but relegated it to an experience of the past.

"Since we have evidence of its existence in the early third century, we can safely assume that its demise occurred between A.D. 250 and 350."[27]

The Long Drought
(A.D. 400-1500)

"From the early fifth century through the entire medieval era, evidences for tongue speaking are scanty at best."[28] J. J. Gorres, in *Die christliche Mystik,* lists a number of people during this period who are credited with speaking in tongues: "St. Anthony of Padua (1195-1231), Ange Clarenua (in 1300), St. Vincent Ferrier (1350-1419), Jeanne of the Cross, St. Francis Xavier (1506-1552), St. Louis Bertrand (1526-1581), and others."[29]

The Cevenols

In southern France around 1685, the Catholic Church began a fresh outburst of persecution against Protestants. In the midst of much violence, a group of peasants in the Cevennes Mountains strongly resisted the pressure to conform. They steadfastly maintained their right to worship according to the dictates of their conscience. As the fervor of persecution increased, reports of spiritual phenomena accompanied it, one being speaking with tongues.

The Irvingites

An eloquent Scottish Presbyterian pastor in London named Edward Irving saw a great outburst of tongues-speaking in the nineteenth century in his Newman Street Church. After witnessing tongues-speaking in Scotland, he returned to his congregation and encouraged the practice there. Tongues broke out in his church in London on April 30, 1831.

Early Revivals

"The seventeenth through the nineteenth centuries were, in fact, particularly fruitful periods for religious enthusiasm in its varied forms. It is difficult to estimate the extent to which glossolalia occurred; however, these popular movements often went unreported or were reported only by detractors."[30]

The Ranters (1648-60), along with large numbers of other sects, practiced speaking in tongues. Little is known about them since they apparently encountered little opposition.

Tongues-speaking was also experienced by the Quakers as one of many expressions of the Spirit's power. "Fox and his followers often reported visions, groaning, quaking or trembling, weeping, outbursts of prophecy, foaming at the mouth, faintings, and the like as a result of their meetings."[31]

Early Methodism also experienced this phenomenon, especially in northern England and Wales. The writings of John Wesley defend the practice against critics. "The Great Awakening and subsequent revivals produced some unusual by-products, of which tongue speaking was undoubtedly one. Spirited preaching, singing, physical movement, and the demand for a tangible display of the receiving of the Spirit worked together to create astounding physical demonstrations."[32]

Latter Rain Outpouring

Charles F. Parham, leader of a small Bible college in Topeka, Kansas, saw the first shower of latter rain on New Year's Day, 1901. Miss Agnes N. Ozman was the first to be baptized in the Holy Ghost with the sign of tongues. On January 3, Parham spoke in tongues along with many students of the school. Students began to evangelize in Kansas, and Parham opened a school in Houston, Texas, in 1905.

Los Angeles was hit with an outpouring in 1906. W. J. Seymour, a black holiness preacher who had studied under Parham, moved his small group into a rented building at 312 Azusa Street. Here they experienced an unusual revival of miracles and saw hundreds receive the baptism in the Holy Ghost with the evidence of speaking in tongues. From here revival spread across America and even took on international proportions. Before the end of 1906, there were Pentecostals in India, Norway and Sweden.

Pentecostalism, with its emphasis upon the baptism in the Holy Ghost, spread as a strong moving force. Several Holiness organizations became Pentecostal, such as the Church of God in Christ and the Pentecostal Holiness Church, and several new Pentecostal organizations were formed, including the United Pentecostal Church and the

Assemblies of God.

The largest of the new Pentecostal organizations is the Assemblies of God with 10,173 churches and a membership of 1,879,182. The largest Oneness organization is the United Pentecostal Church International with 3,300 churches and 465,000 members."[33]

The Charismatic Movement

The Full Gospel Businessmen's Fellowship International was born in 1951 under the inspiration of a wealthy California dairyman Demos Shakarian and healing evangelist Oral Roberts. Through the 1950's and 1960's this organization had great influence upon non-Pentecostal businessmen. Many non-Pentecostal ministers began to receive the Holy Ghost and speak in tongues. Many ministers were dismissed from their pastorates as a result, and received wide publicity around the world.

The Jesus Movement of the 1960's was largely neo-Pentecostal. The tongues-speaking experience began to cross over denominational lines. Many neo-Pentecostal leaders emerged from within the traditional denominations. The experience spread to every major denomination including the Roman Catholic Church. The *Minneapolis Tribune* on June 12, 1978, reported that the charismatic movement "has an estimated five million Catholic adherents in the United States" alone.

Our day has seen the most widespread and most far-reaching outpouring of the baptism in the Holy Ghost that has ever been witnessed.

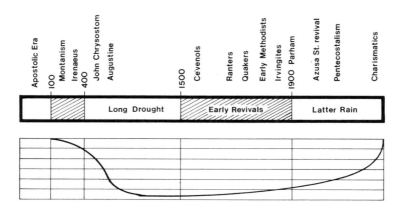

Tongues in History

CONCLUSION

From a survey of church history, we see a decline from the original doctrine and experience at the end of the first century. Christendom progressively distanced itself from the original until it reached a nadir just prior to the Reformation. The Reformation began a progressive movement back to the Apostolic Church pattern. The progress continues even to the present-day outpouring of the Spirit.

This latter-day revival must be the fulfillment of Joel's promise:

> "For he hath given you the former rain moderately, and he will cause to come down for you the rain, the former rain, and the latter rain . . . . And the floors shall be full of wheat, and the fats shall overflow with wine and oil" (Joel 2:23-24).

172

It is also the continuing and more complete fulfillment of Joel 2:28: "And it shall come to pass afterward, that I will pour out my spirit upon all flesh."

We are seeing a great return in our present world to the biblical new birth experience witnessed by blood, water and Spirit. Many once again believe in repentance, water baptism in the name of Jesus Christ, the baptism of the Holy Ghost with the evidence of speaking with other tongues, and living a holy life. According to the *World Christian Encyclopedia* in 1970 there were 13,350 Oneness Pentecostal churches worldwide with 1,593,999 adult members, 2,682,248 in total affiliation, and a projection of 4,205,428 in affiliation by 1985."[34]

FOOTNOTES

[1]Lars P. Qualbon, *A History of the Christian Church* (New York: T. Nelson, 1958), pp. 86, 96.

[2]James Hastings, ed., *Encyclopedia of Religion and Ethics,* II, 734.

[3]Tim Dowley, ed., *Eerdman's Handbook of the History of Christianity* (Grand Rapids: Eerdmans, 1977), p. 400.

[4]Charles P. Schmitt, *Root out of a Dry Ground* (Grand Rapids: Fellowship Publications, 1979), p. 107.

[5]Dowley, ed., p. 111.

[6]Schmitt, p. 119.

[7]"Baptism," *Encyclopedia Britannica* (1937), III, 82.

[8] Williston Walker, *A History of the Christian Church* (New York:

Charles Scribner's Sons, 1918), p.94.

[9]*Ibid.*

[10]*Ibid.,* p. 95.

[11]Jerald C. Braver, *Dictionary of Church History,* p. 83.

[12]*Encyclopedia Britannica* (1937), III, 84.

[13]*Ibid.,* p. 85.

[14]Dowley, ed., p. 399.

[15]*Ibid.,* p. 480.

[16]*World Book Encyclopedia* (1985), II, 70-71.

[17]Walker, p. 96

[18]*Ibid.*

[19]"Baptism," *Encyclopedia Americana* (Dunbury: Grolier, 1980), III, 208.

[20]"Baptism," *Encyclopedia of the Lutheran Church* (Minneapolis: Augsbury Publishing House, 1965), I, 188.

[21]Louis LaRavoire Morrow, *My Catholic Faith* (Kenosha, Wis.: My Mission House, 1961), p. 270.

[22]"Baptism," *Encylopedia Britannica* (1937), III, 82.

[23]David Bernard, *The Oneness of God* (Hazelwood, Mo.; Word Aflame Press, 1983), p. 277.

[24]Walker, p. 95.

[25]*Encyclopedia Britannica* (1937), III, 83.

[26]E. Glenn Hinson, *Glossolalia* (Nashville: Abingdon, 1967), p. 53.

[27]*Ibid.*

[28]*Ibid.,* p. 56.

[29]George Cotten, ed., *Speaking with Tongues* (New Haven: Yale University Press, 1927), pp. 37-40.

[30]Hinson, p. 63.

[31]*Ibid.*

[32]*Ibid.,* p. 65

[33]*The World Almanac* (New York: Newspaper Enterprise Association, 1985), p. 357.

[34]David Barrett, ed., *World Christian Encyclopedia* (1982), pp. 792-93.

11.

Promise, Principle, Problem, Provision

*W*hen a person is born again, the excitement he experiences is absolutely wonderful. He staggers around as if drunk on new wine. The "delivery room" is filled with his new brothers and sisters who add to the joy with their shouts and prayers. Fresh out of the baptistry, the new convert's hair is still wet from the watery grave. Everyone's attention is focused on him. He is engulfed with bear hugs and greetings of "Praise the Lord." He is counted as one of those who made the evangelistic service or revival a success. At that moment he is just a babe in Christ. Just a simple word of testimony from him is enough to set off a volley of rejoicing among the saints.

The new convert feels so powerful. With the emotional surge and with all the love and support, he may suppose that living for God is going to be absolutely free of problems and trials. His entrance into the kingdom of God is so glorious that it is easy for him to become disoriented. He may not realize that he has just volunteered for service in God's army and is about to be shipped to boot camp.

The conversion experience of repentance, baptism and receiving of the Holy Spirit is not the end of God's plan for man, but the beginning. The Word of God calls it a "new birth." The new convert is newly born, and must now grow to maturity, encountering the problems and vicissitudes of life. The conversion experience is the foundation of a building, of which God is the architect. It is the resurrection of a little seed that, if nurtured properly, will become a strong and fruitful plant.

An erroneous and dangerous attitude for a new Christian to take is thinking, "Now I am saved and my responsibility ends here." People with this mentality think all they need to do is "hold the fort" and wait for rescue through an escape hatch called the rapture. This can be called "waiting-for-the-rapture syndrome." These Christians often do not seem to rejoice unless they are singing a song about heaven. They are just "enduring to the end." They may be saved, but they are miserable all the while.

However, serving the Lord is the most challenging and exciting adventure in life. It affects every facet of existence. Our experience with God involves many cycles and stages of growth—times of great thirst for God and times of struggle to maintain a devotional life; times of great emotion and times of emotional dryness; times of blessing and times of suffering; times of victory and times of apparent defeat; times of fervent activity and times of rest; times of fellowship and times of solitude.

As new citizens of the kingdom of God, many promises become ours. Someone has said there are over 700 promises in the Word of God. Undoubtedly, there are promises we have not even grasped yet! We have more promises than we realize!

It is important to understand, however, that promises are not substance. They are like tokens that are useless unless they are redeemed by meeting certain conditions. Everything God has given us comes in promise form. All of these promises are redeemed through faith. Faith is the battering ram which breaks through circumstances, removing obstacles that prevent us from receiving our inheritance.

God wants to take us into a spiritual land flowing with milk and honey, where we live in a perpetual climate of victory, claiming our inheritance of righteousness, peace and joy in the Holy Ghost (Romans 14:17).

It was not God's will just to get Israel out of Egypt; He wanted to lead them into a land of their own. "And he brought us out from thence, that he might bring us in, to give us the land which he sware unto our fathers" (Deuteronomy 6:23).

There is a cycle or process repeated over and over again in God's dealings with man to bring him into his rightful inheritance in the plan of God: *Promise—Principle—Problem—Provision*. Let us consider one example of this process—the deliverance of the Israelites from Egypt and their progression towards the Promise Land.

PROMISE

First of all, Chapter 3, has shown how blood, water and Spirit witnessed in their deliverance. Blood was applied to the doorpost to protect them from the death angel. The crossing of the Red Sea provided the witness of water. And the pillar of cloud and pillar of fire gave the witness of the Spirit. This is a type of repentence, baptism and receiving the Holy Ghost.

This aspect of their experience is the *Promise*. Moses told them that God wanted to set them free. Not only that, He wanted to give them their own land—a land so abundantly fertile that He described it as a "land flowing with milk and honey."

When a person has just been born again, he is at the stage of Promise. Romans 8, for instance, gives a whole spectrum of promises to the child of God, such as freedom from condemnation, freedom from the law of sin and death, life, peace, resurrection power, being joint-heirs with Christ, and the intercession of the Spirit. There are at least twenty-one promises in this chapter alone.

PRINCIPLE

For every promise God has given, there is an *if*. Israel was promised "great and goodly cities, which thou buildest not. . .wells digged, which thou diggedst not, vineyards and olive trees, which thou plantest not" (Deuteronomy 6:10-11). With these promises, God gave a strong warning: "Then beware lest thou forget the LORD, which brought thee forth out of the land of Egypt, from the house of bondage. Thou shalt fear the LORD thy God, and serve him, and shalt swear by his name" (Deuteronomy 6:12-13). With many other words, the Lord exhorted and instructed them about being faithful to His commandments and statutes.

The Israelites camped at Mt. Sinai for approximately eleven months. With earthquakes, supernatural sounds, fire and smoke, God visited His people and gave them the law, the priesthood, and the Tabernacle. This was the *Principle* stage of their journey. They now had a written law, a church, and a ministry.

A new convert who is fed too strong of a diet of Promise and not enough Principle will become frustrated and disoriented. Many have perished when they discovered that their new "Bless Me Club" did not work as they thought it should. Just to take the promise and not the principle is to be presumptuous.

PROBLEM

If it were not for the *Problem* stage, the Christian life would be "cotton candy religion" with a "get-rich-quick" plan. The rush of new converts would overwhelm the church as they clamored for a slice of the pie. We would become a very selfish and indulgent people who would forget God. With a magic formula for success, we would soon depart from true spirituality, worship and dependence on God.

Israel left Mt. Sinai fully equipped to take the land. They camped at Kadesh-Barnea and sent twelve spies into the land. The spies confirmed that the land was greatly to be desired. But there was a problem. The walls of the cities were thick and high, and there were giants in the land. The spies vividly described themselves as grasshoppers compared to the Canaanites. The negative report of the ten spies overpowered the faith of the two spies, who gave a good report, and Israel's faith was poisoned.

A person may have the most wonderful conversion experience, with visions, goosebumps, voices, and hours of talking in tongues. He may have the largest and most expensive Bible available. In times of trial, temptation or crises, however, the crucial questions are "How much of the Word does he have in his heart?" and "How strong is his faith in the Word?"

There are three choices in the face of Problem:

1. Return to the wilderness where it is safer and remain there with the "hold-the-fort" group, resolving that certain promises are not for us and harboring a defeatist attitude.

181

2. Retreat temporarily and try again later.

3. Stand. This is the correct choice. "Wherefore take unto you the whole armour of God, that ye may be able to withstand in the evil day, and having done all, to stand" (Ephesians 6:13).

PROVISION

Because of unbelief, Israel turned back to the wilderness and wandered aimlessly for forty years. God provided for their sustenance with manna; their clothes did not grow old nor did their feet swell for forty years (Deuteronomy 8:4). That 3,000,000 people lived in a desert for forty years is a miracle. But desert living was not the ultimate in God's plan for them.

When Israel conquered Canaan under the leadership of Joshua, they were an entirely different group of people. There were only two men over sixty years old, Joshua and Caleb. All of the older ones had died and were buried in the Sinai Peninsula. The crossing over the Jordan River marked the entering into *Provision*. The Lord enabled Israel to take the land. They began to live in houses they had not built to gather grapes from vineyards they had not planted, and to draw water from wells they had not dug. God still required obedience—the Principle did not change —but life in the land of Canaan was quite a change from life in the wilderness.

It is the will of God that we prosper spiritually, financially, physically and emotionally. However, our witness to the world consists not only in how strictly we comply with certain moral rules, but also in our prevailing attitude in the face of financial difficulty, health emergencies, emotional stress and challenges to our faith.

In the final analysis, prosperity or poverty does not prove anything about a person's spirituality. The important thing is his attitude about his situation. Everyone has a different role to play in life. One person's financial status will differ from someone else's, as well as skills, talents, and IQ. Regardless of our place in God's creative genius, we should strive to improve every facet of our person and to reach out to others in a redemptive way.

Note: The main ideas in this chapter are taken from The Purpose of Temptation (Fleming H. Revell Company, Old Tappan, NJ. 1973) by Bob Mumford and used, with his permission.

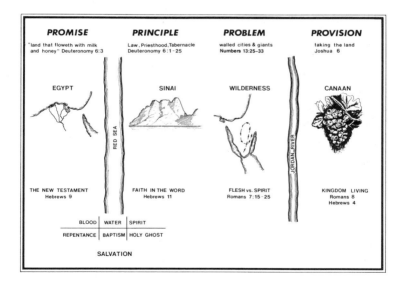